Friendship and Resistance

Eberhard Bethge

Friendship
and Resistance

**Essays on
Dietrich
Bonhoeffer**

WCC Publications, Geneva

*William B. Eerdmans Publishing Company
Grand Rapids, Michigan*

Published jointly 1995 by WCC Publications, Geneva, and by
Wm. B. Eerdmans Publishing Co.
255 Jefferson Ave. S.E., Grand Rapids, Michigan 49503

Printed in the United States of America

00 99 98 97 96 95   7 6 5 4 3 2 1

ISBN 2-8254-1153-1 (WCC)
ISBN 0-8028-4123-6 (Eerdmans)

Cover design by Rob Lucas

Contents

The Bonhoeffer Family

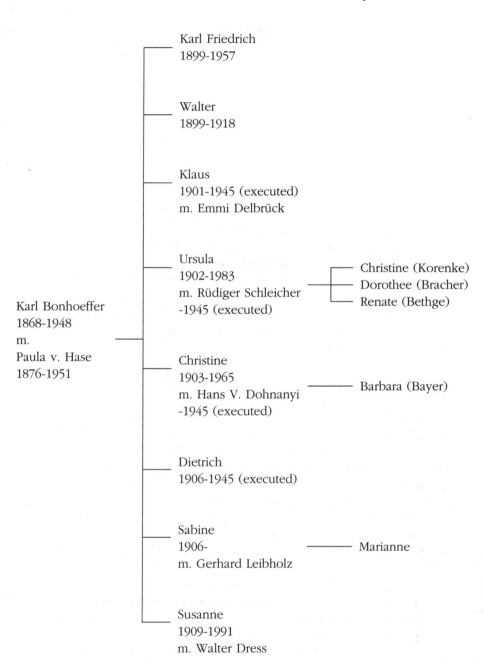

Karl Friedrich
1899-1957

Walter
1899-1918

Klaus
1901-1945 (executed)
m. Emmi Delbrück

Ursula
1902-1983
m. Rüdiger Schleicher
-1945 (executed)

Christine (Korenke)
Dorothee (Bracher)
Renate (Bethge)

Karl Bonhoeffer
1868-1948
m.
Paula v. Hase
1876-1951

Christine
1903-1965
m. Hans V. Dohnanyi
-1945 (executed)

Barbara (Bayer)

Dietrich
1906-1945 (executed)

Sabine
1906-
m. Gerhard Leibholz

Marianne

Susanne
1909-1991
m. Walter Dress

Preface

This small volume brings together for the first time in English some writings of Eberhard Bethge, perhaps one of the least known among the great ecumenical witnesses of our time. As a belated gift and tribute for his 85th birthday on August 28, 1994, this publication is an expression of gratitude for what the ecumenical movement has received through and from Eberhard Bethge. Why such an explicit tribute to someone who is hardly known outside his own country Germany?

The first and most important reason is linked with the person and the legacy of Dietrich Bonhoeffer. Bonhoeffer's seminal influence on the ecumenical movement and his close association and friendship with such early ecumenical leaders as Bishop George Bell, W.A. Visser 't Hooft, Paul Lehmann and others are well-known. However, most of what we know about Bonhoeffer has come to us through Eberhard Bethge. It was he who edited Bonhoeffer's letters from prison, which have had an impact worldwide on successive generations of Christians and theologians. He collected and made available Bonhoeffer's writings, the first volume of which carries the title *Ökumene*. He gave many years of his life to preparing what is recognized as the definitive biography of Bonhoeffer, including a penetrating interpretation of his continuing significance for the ecumenical movement. Even the formation of the International Bonhoeffer Society, which has become a vital instrument for ecumenical theological exchange and reflection, and the creation of an ecumenically oriented Dietrich Bonhoeffer Chair at Union Theological Seminary in New York owe their existence in large measure to Eberhard Bethge. He is a precious example of an interpreter/biographer who, by identifying fully with his friend and asking no recognition for himself, has emerged all the more clearly as a powerful prophetic voice in his own right.

The second reason is that Eberhard Bethge has quietly and patiently begun to teach us a new language for church and theology. This is the language of "confession and resistance", the language of "deed and suffering", a language of truth and "creative shame", which faces the burden of two thousand years of Christian imperialism, especially towards the Jewish people. Bethge learned the "alphabet" of this new language from Bonhoeffer, but he gained mastery in it through his own intensive participation in Jewish-Christian dialogue. As an old man, he finds it difficult to change. He has discovered how deep a transformation of the traditional Christian consciousness is required to learn and speak this new language and that it will take several generations to mature.

The third reason is related to Bethge's life-long commitment to active commemoration and his struggle against blindness and forgetfulness. His rediscovery of the old insight that "commemoration renders life human; forgetfulness makes it inhuman" and that "remembrance... fills the future with perspectives" is of great ecumenical significance. In fact, the reconciliation of memories has become one of the most urgent tasks in the search for unity and koinonia — among peoples as well as among churches. But healing and reconciliation do not come from denial of the past with its pain and hurt and from an exclusive focus on the present; it is only through active remembrance of and accountability for the past that the space is opened up for a new tomorrow. Eberhard Bethge has dedicated his whole life to active remembrance of the past in order to redeem our painful and divided heritage and to "offer us space to breathe". He has given us an example of how tradition, instead of tying us to the past, can in fact liberate us for facing the future, an important lesson as we approach the end of a millennium which has been so shaped by Christian division.

The essays assembled in this small volume reflect these three commitments of Bethge's life. They are partly biographical, but they open perspectives which are of immediate significance for the ecumenical movement in its present predicament. They have been selected by Werner Simpfendörfer, who has inspired and promoted this publication. May this tribute to Eberhard Bethge make his voice heard more widely for the benefit of the worldwide ecumenical movement.   *Konrad Raiser*

Chapter 1

The Chronicler of an Era

Clemens Vollnhals: *Professor Bethge, you are primarily known to a broad public as the author of the definitive biography of Dietrich Bonhoeffer, your friend and teacher. Alongside your job as a pastor, you have devoted your life to editing Bonhoeffer's unpublished works and managing his estate. You yourself were born on August 28, 1909, and your father was a United Lutheran pastor. Can you tell us a bit about your background? Was it just something natural for you to follow in his footsteps and become a pastor yourself?*

Eberhard Bethge: It was the most natural thing in the world. I grew up in a tiny village, and my first conscious impressions were my pride in my father. As the pastor of a Lutheran congregation of farmers in a Prussian village — all his equals, of course — he seemed to me like the king of the village who knew everything, who stood up above us in the pulpit, who talked with the village dignitaries and was sought out by them. I was terribly proud of him. And when he died very young — I was only 14 — I made a vow to myself to follow in his footsteps. I have never regretted this decision. There were periods when I certainly thought I would like to gain other kinds of experience, but the decision remained firm. So did the impression of this father with whom I never had a critical relationship due to his death. This impression has marked my whole life.

A radio interview broadcast on August 23, 1989.

Vollnhals: *And so you never regretted this decision?*

Bethge: Loyalty to my father and to myself could never have really allowed that. Of course, when I went to boarding school in town I came to know a totally new life and did things that were actually outside the little world of a village parsonage and its values. I enjoyed doing new things, even wrong things, in order to experience something of the world. Yet despite this urbanization in my own life I never departed from my aim of becoming a pastor.

Vollnhals: *You were a young theology student when you joined up with the Confessing Church. How did that happen?*

Bethge: It does seem strange that in 1933 my friends and I were so clear in our support for the opposition of the time, the Young Reforming Movement, which grew into the Confessing Church. We never hesitated for a moment. During my childhood in the second German Reich, the greatest thing that could happen to me was when my father would drive us children to Potsdam once a year — Potsdam, with its Garrison Church and memorials to Frederick the Great, with the soldiers singing "Now thank we all our God" after the Prussian defeat of the Austrians in 1757. Those are very strong, lasting childhood impressions, which were the reason why we at first welcomed the political events of 1933. And yet my student friends and I, who all came from the same area, were perfectly clear that the Confessing Church was the right one, and that Hitler just did not know what it was and needed to be better informed by his advisors. And we dreamed that Karl Barth might have a word with him some time and then everything would be different. We were certainly labouring under an illusion. But for at least two years, if not three, we thought we could live with the new political regime in Germany and should even support it; yet we knew we needed to stand up to the church authorities and the Nazification of church teaching.

Vollnhals: *Membership of the Confessing Church had serious consequences for you. You were expelled from the Wittenberg seminary and fell in with Bonhoeffer. How did you feel as an "illegal" young theologian of the Confessing Church? That was* *quite a new step, which led so far away from state Protestantism that you were also in opposition to the regime.*

Bethge: I don't think that we actually saw our expulsion from the Wittenberg seminary in October 1934 as a gesture against the Third Reich and the new state. We still thought that we were resisting a misguided *Reichsbischof*[1] and a wrongheaded church government both in Berlin and in Magdeburg, our own province, and that we had to resist for the sake of Germany, and we had to disobey.

At the time, in October 1934, the Confessing Church was holding its second big synod in Dahlem, Berlin, in which it declared that these heretical, Nazified church leaders should not be obeyed and emergency bodies should be set up to replace them. We students leaped at the opportunity, having waited six months already for such a statement. We challenged the seminary director to follow the Dahlem Synod decision and place the whole seminary under the Confessing Church. He didn't do that, of course, and promptly reported us and our proposal. The next morning the telegram came from the bishop that we were to be expelled.

There were 15 of us, out of 20 to 25 candidates, who actually had to pack up and leave. That meant that we had left the jurisdiction of the official church, the Magdeburg church authorities. We could not yet grasp the full implications of that, of course. We did understand that a totally new period would follow and that we would have to make sacrifices. But the Confessing Church in Saxony welcomed us with open arms: those who had been thrown out had to be accommodated with pastors of the Confessing Church as assistant pastors, and that kept us going for the moment. The students who did not go along with us certainly missed out on a whole new field of experience. That was what we thought. It may have been naive sometimes. And we were a great burden to the pastors in the Confessing Church, who had to support us financially as well. But we had a clear conscience and felt very good about it.

Vollnhals: *What was your first impression of Bonhoeffer when you started attending the newly founded seminary of the Confessing Church?*

Bethge: After our practical training in local churches, we waited until the Confessing Church could arrange for us to complete our course before our final exams, seeing that we had been excluded from the official theology degree. It was six months before we heard from the new church authority, the *Bruderrat*,[2] that we should go to Berlin and report to the person responsible for this final stage of training for the Confessing candidates, Wilhelm Niesel, a very good fellow. We were supposed to pick up our instructions there. Later I heard that I had been initially assigned to a seminary on the Rhine, but that this had been changed at the last minute. I was then told to go to Pomerania, and report to the makeshift seminary located at Zingst on the Baltic coast. The director was Dietrich Bonhoeffer. I think this was the first time I heard his name. I did not know of his theological significance, or what he had been up to during the first couple of years of the church struggle. From fellow students who had also been sent from the Berlin church I heard that we could consider ourselves lucky to have been assigned to study with him.

I turned up in the evening, a day later than the others, and I looked around to find out who the director was. He was barely distinguishable as such. Most of us were almost the same age as he was, so someone had to point him out. He came to greet me, and to my amazement invited me to go for a walk along the beach with him. As we walked up and down he asked me what I had gone through so far in the church struggle, where I came from, and about my family and friends. This taking a personal interest from the start was quite new to me, as compared to the theological teachers I had met before.

The next morning we heard the first lecture. And the first lectures we heard were what later made Bonhoeffer famous, his lectures on the Sermon on the Mount, published as *The Cost of Discipleship*. He interpreted the Reformation message in a way that was quite new to us, and we even protested a bit when he suddenly made concepts interchangeable which we had learned to distinguish, such as faith and obedience: first comes faith, faith, faith and then perhaps obedience. From Bonhoeffer I first heard the famous phrase: "Only believers obey and only the obedient believe." And dealing with the early Reformation's *sola gratia* ("by grace alone") in the field of reality in which one has faith, the actual, everyday life of one's own context, was quite new to us and made a deep impression.

This man with his great theological training was the resolute representative of the Confessing Church that we students expected our teachers to be. And this resolute teacher was also extremely musical. He was a gifted pianist and loved 19th-century music; he was a great Beethoven player and he could sit down at the piano and simply improvise the *Rosenkavalier*. That impressed us greatly. Also he was good at sport and had a strong, well-developed physique. He hated to lose when we tried shot-putting, or stone-putting, down on the beach.

Vollnhals: *You then became Bonhoeffer's assistant and followed his activities at close range. What effect did it have on you when you heard that Bonhoeffer was now moving from opposition within the church to political resistance to the Nazi regime, and that he was involved in the Hitler plot, a conspirator against the powers-that-be in the traditional Lutheran sense? What did you think and how did you react?*

Bethge: That was something that took years to lead up to. But there were way-stations in this process. The first amazing event happened when we were with him at the beach for four or five days in May. We heard Hitler speaking on the radio from Tempelhofer Feld in Berlin. He referred in this address to the great historic events by which Germany had now regained respect in the world and the German nation was being renewed — for example, the Day of Potsdam[3] and May 16, 1935, when universal military service was introduced. As Hitler mentioned these events I noticed that Bonhoeffer reacted with disapproval, not to say absolute rejection, of these things which my friends and I had completely accepted as a way of showing our patriotic convictions. When we asked him why, he said we should talk about it that evening. And then for the first time I saw a Lutheran theologian in the tradition of the Reformation talk like a pacifist. He spoke of how he thought there should be something like pure and simple obedience to the commandment of the Sermon on the Mount and there should also be the option for a Christian not to take up arms. He spoke without any fanaticism, but we were amazed, as we had never been taught like that in our whole course of studies.

Another very important way-station was naturally November 9, 1938,[4] although it passed uneventfully for us. We were in East Pomerania at the time, holding training courses (illegally) in a village where there were no Jews or storm troopers. And it was probably only the next day that we heard on the radio what had taken place all over the Reich. Bonhoeffer then phoned his family in the code language usual at the time to find out what had happened.

In the second half of our training programme, in the town of Köslin, Bonhoeffer heard that the synagogue there had been burned down. This had nothing to do with God's wrath regarding the Jews, he told us, nor was it a punishment of any kind. Now that synagogues had burned, the churches would be next. And then in our devotions, which took the form of sitting silently in prayer and meditation about a certain biblical verse, he drew our attention to Psalm 74. I don't know how he hit upon it, but it says, "They have burned up all the synagogues of God in the land." He wrote to all the candidates for ordination, trying to show them that something had happened here for which we would have to pay and that the role of a pastor preaching grace from the pulpit every Sunday would never be the same again.

Bonhoeffer himself had made a conscious decision to become a pastor, in a large family with a liberal sprinkling of lawyers, doctors and even politicians. Initially he had thought he could leave it to them to restrain or remove Hitler, or to prevent certain things from happening, or even to plan a coup at some stage. He had seen his mission as being in the church. But now it was clear to him that the church could not be silent in this matter. There were only political courses open; it was primarily a matter of taking political steps, since the totalitarian state, the dictatorship, had developed in such a way that an underground organization was necessary in order to stop Hitler. This idea was developed from 1938 until it saw the light of day on July 20, 1944, when these endeavours finally proved to have failed.

I myself grew into this milieu only very slowly, starting in Berlin, through becoming friends with Bonhoeffer, and even marrying his niece. Then of course I fully belonged, albeit on the fringe. That was a long path. It was suddenly clear to me that it was not enough to preach with conviction. Now people were being killed in their thousands and that had to be stopped. It was an unforgivable sin to let that happen, even more unforgivable than to take part in a plot to kill Hitler.

Vollnhals: *You yourself were arrested in October 1944 and spent the last months in the Gestapo dungeons in Berlin as an accessory after the fact. On May 8, 1945, you were literally liberated by the Russian troops. How did you experience the actual end of the war? For most of the German population it was not a day of liberation but more one of humiliating defeat. You yourself were then let out of prison. What was your impression of the general atmosphere?*

Bethge: In fact, my "May 8", so to speak, was April 25. On that day, at four o'clock in the afternoon, our guards opened the prison doors and let us out. They had taken over from the SS guards during the previous day, and so were now normal prison officials. We could hear the Russian machine guns that day, and tried to explain to them that when the first Russians came they would kill them rather than us. So they let us out, and we marched home, not terribly happily actually, since people had been disappearing from our prison day by day. Both my father-in-law and Bonhoeffer's brother Klaus, who were in the same prison, had disappeared two nights earlier. Soon afterwards we learned that they had been summarily shot amid the rubble in Berlin.

And yet, we had survived, we had been spared. I don't think we could really grasp what that meant at first. The homecoming was overwhelming. We were hardly able to imagine that things could simply pick up from the time before 1933, in the church and even more so in politics. That was not possible for us who had a bit of an idea of what had happened to the Jews; we did not have the exact facts and figures, of course — although the Bonhoeffer family did know quite a bit. We simply could not imagine another Germany just starting up again as if nothing had happened since 1933. It took a while before it was clear to us that just that was probably going to happen after all; at least people were trying it and even those with responsibility, who knew where the money was, and knew their way around the law, the ins-and-outs of the church and the constitution, had precisely that in mind.

You could see and feel it — as if things like concentration camps and the annihilation of the Jews had almost completely escaped them or they had simply closed their minds to it all. It is very strange indeed that the first important postwar statement by the church, the Stuttgart confession of guilt, does not explicitly mention the annihilation of the Jews. It is undeniable that people knew a bit about it already. And they obviously thought about these things in Stuttgart, on that mountain of rubble. But that a complete turnaround was necessary for theology and the church, and also for Germany, going deeper than ever before, was probably not yet clear in the period immediately following May 8, 1945.

Vollnhals: *This realization came very, very late. But immediately after your release you suddenly became the personal assistant of Bishop Dibelius, a man who wanted to pick up where he had had to stop in 1933, and who in the view of the Confessing Church leadership was a restorer, while you were a member of the Unterwegskreis,⁵ a reformist wing that now had quite different ideas of the way the church should go. Didn't it sometimes make your relationship to Dibelius a bit tense that your ideas were so divergent? And did you sometimes get the feeling that an historic chance to make a new beginning was being missed?*

Bethge: With time we certainly did realize that. But the *Unterwegskreis*, the group of so-called "young brothers" who had been illegal and were now recognized pastors, only started up in 1946. And that Dibelius was such an advocate of restoration became clear to us only later — at least we did not want to admit it at first.

I spent the first few weeks of May in Berlin cycling around to try to find out what had happened to my own relatives, particularly my wife's relatives, on the Bonhoeffer side, my father-in-law and others, or where they had been killed. I visited my old director in the Gossner Mission in Berlin, and he told me that a new church government was being set up. Dibelius was a vital, clever, resolute man, who had set up a new church administrative body as early as May 7 in the Burckhardt Haus in Berlin. He got moving as none of the others did. And my old boss from the Gossner Mission, with whom I had worked at the beginning of the war after the seminary had been closed, said, "Go along and see him. You know that someone has to start putting order into chaos." And Dibelius was the man.

When I turned up at his office in mid-May I met none of the old *Bruderrat* people, not Martin Alberts and not Hans Böhm or any of the others we had known and revered, but Otto Dibelius instead. And the first thing he said was, "Brother Bethge, you stay here, right here in my office." You have to understand that for us in the church struggle Otto Dibelius was not only a restorationist, an old-style Prussian Lutheran, but he had been part of both the Barmen and the Dahlem Synods in 1934. He had been the only general superintendent to be deposed, had moved into a shabby apartment in Lichterfeld and had remained a member of the *Bruderrat* all through the years.

In May and during the whole of 1945 we still felt a sense of solidarity with a man like Dibelius. He was the man who had helped to protect us, who had backed us up in our illegal situation. Although in the 1920s he had made a clearly anti-Semitic statement, he had also been one of those who had assisted Jews in hiding. We have proof of that. So in 1945 there was no break yet between him and us younger ones, who were still expecting certain things to happen. There was an overwhelmingly strong desire to work together in the church in the chaotic situation of Berlin at the time, and that is what I did.

From the start Dibelius promised to give me every opportunity to do what needed to be done for the Bonhoeffer family. I wanted to investigate the fate of Dietrich Bonhoeffer, specifically the manner of his death, and see to the preservation and administration of his estate. As Dibelius's assistant I accompanied him to the West — to Treysa, Frankfurt and Stuttgart — and in October to the first Council meetings of the newly forming Evangelical Church in Germany. But I didn't attend many of the discussions because I regarded it as my main task to shed light on the fate of Dietrich Bonhoeffer. It took a long time until we found out the facts, until the end of July 1945.

Vollnhals: *Soon afterwards you started compiling and editing unpublished writings, particularly* Ethics, *which appeared in 1949. There was astonishingly little response, and interest in Bonhoeffer developed relatively late in fact. Did that embitter you?*

Bethge: No, not immediately. It only showed me how difficult it is to arouse sympathy for someone who has tried to think out something new. At first only I knew what he had written to me in his letters from prison. And I was a young man, a small fish in the Berlin church. It was pretty difficult to gain a hearing. And it took four years until it was possible to read his ideas in *Ethics* and another five to six years until the *Letters and Papers from Prison* appeared, which did create a sensation, in Germany and the rest of the world. And this sensation has not died down to this day. But it is indeed odd that Bonhoeffer's theological, ethical and general statements are still disturbing for the church — the church that simply picked up the threads from before 1933.

Vollnhals: *Later, in 1953, you went to London for eight years as a pastor to the German congregation there. Why was that? Had you begun to despair at the turn the church was taking in Germany? Why did you leave?*

Bethge: I don't think I had given up hope yet. I think it was only much later that I had to resign myself to the fact that the period of the Confessing Church had changed very little. Prior to that we still thought that what we had experienced so fundamentally during the Nazi period in the Confessing Church, during the resistance, would catch on. I was still very hopeful. It was very strange.

In 1953 Niemöller came to see me. He was responsible for ecumenical relations and also for churches and congregations abroad. He asked whether I would take a post in London, one that Bonhoeffer had held himself. That was attraction enough. The other reason was that Dibelius came and asked, "Don't you want to go to London? We want the present pastor back here in Berlin and you can take his place." It was a totally new world for me, and I was curious to see what it would be like. It was very important to have done it, I think. For the first time I experienced my own Evangelical Lutheran congregational work in the context of a free church. We existed legally in London, but as a tiny free church in a free church system, which was quite different from our *Volkskirche* situation in Germany.

No, I was still hopeful at the time, not yet disillusioned at our having achieved so little.

Vollnhals: *After your return you took over leadership of a seminary yourself, the pastoral college of the Rhineland Church. What were your most important goals in your work? Particularly, what was your experience with the student rebellion of 1968, the start of a new, different generation of theologians?*

Bethge: Coming back from abroad in 1961 to work in the Rhineland Church was of course a very important step. I did not return to Berlin, nor to my real home, the province of Saxony, but went to a church which we had always regarded as a particularly fine, well-functioning church. The Rhenish Confessing Church had a very good reputation. And now it called me to conduct in-service training for pastors. This was another chance for me to prove myself, a real challenge. I was convinced that it was an important opportunity and that I could perhaps bring in the concerns of Bonhoeffer.

I worked in that field for 14 years and got to know the Rhineland for the very first time, from the inside. And it was not as perfect as we used to think. But I was a part of the major change in emphasis that took place in pastoral in-service training. When I arrived the issues were still exegesis, hermeneutics — questions like those raised by Rudolf Bultmann. And for the first four or five years the topics of our courses for pastors centred on questions of exegesis and exposition. Then there was a switch to issues of social ethics, which predominated in the next four or five years. Then the trend was towards sensitivity training, reflecting the new interest in psychology as preparation for pastoral work. In this way I had to go through changes I never dreamed of, having been brought up on the theology of Karl Barth.

Vollnhals: *This was the period of what one could call your second life-project, the intensive work on Christian-Jewish reconciliation, also your criticism of the church's late assimilation of its past. In an article you once spoke of the imperialist language of Christianity towards Judaism. What did you mean by that?*

Bethge: I mean the process by which it suddenly became clear that for centuries *we* defined who were Jews and how they were Jews, without listening and talking to the Jews themselves. In our university courses and professional training, the history of the Jews usually ended with the destruction of Jerusalem in the year

70. Modern, present-day Judaism as such hardly existed at all. It is amazing that neither Barth nor Bonhoeffer nor any other of our great teachers ever took us to visit a synagogue. We did not even know what that would be like. The need to work through what we had done to the Jews by keeping silent or standing by at Auschwitz was a realization that got through to us amazingly late.

I think that two things helped me to clarify my perception. First there was my time spent with Dietrich Bonhoeffer, who from 1933 was not just concerned with the problem of baptized Jews within the church but always saw the problem of the Jews as such, that is, anti-Semitism, as the core problem of Nazism. It was important for me that I was close to him and somehow internalized and absorbed his first steps on this path. Second, there was the fact that I had come across emigrants during my time in London. I got to know their everyday lives, their great difficulty in having to change their identity, to lose the one they had had in Germany and to find a new one. I saw the crises and the problems very clearly.

I got involved with the beginnings of the German dialogue, the nascent dialogue between churches, Christians, theologians and Jews, survivors whose lives had been saved, who came and talked with us, which was not to be expected at all. I started with all that on my return from Britain, and even then very late. Suddenly I was invited to the working group and the *Kirchentag*;[6] then I frequently went to the United States and attended the first holocaust conferences. I had the feeling at home in Germany that I was talking about things which were absolutely new and not perceived at all by Christians there.

Vollnhals: *Your call for a theological revision of Christian doctrine does not meet with approval everywhere. How do you judge the future prospects of the Christian-Jewish dialogue?*

Bethge: A certain phase of enthusiasm has just come to an end here, I would say. The discovery of how strongly my Christian faith draws on its Jewish roots, the discovery that the figure of Jesus Christ is not a divisive one but one which bonds me with the Jews — that was such a strong theological impulse that one can perhaps forgive a certain euphoria, and understand how it came about. When you have grasped that and when Jews have really been able to show you how strongly Jewish the gospels are, such enthusiasm is quite understandable.

Now, however, we are coming to a critical point, at which the church is the actual addressee of the Christian-Jewish dialogue. I don't believe that the Jews have to change. It is the churches which have to, and they will have to change something that is a thousand years old. In order to do this they will need several generations, not just one. We will have to change our language completely. I am an old man and it is very hard to have to learn a new language. But I see with great joy now that young theology students and assistant pastors are starting to do this by going to Israel to study for a year. That offers great possibilities for change. Yet I can understand that people initially feel insecure and prefer to cling to the old ways.

Vollnhals: *One final question. What has actually happened to the hopes of the illegal young theologians of the Confessing Church? What hopes have been fulfilled and what changes are still to come, when you look back over your 80 years of life and the way the church has developed in Germany?*

Bethge: This is not an easy question to answer. I have mixed feelings about it all. I cannot and will not deny my decisive years, in which I was filled with theological renewal, with the renewal of knowing how and why I am a Christian. And I still believe today that the Christ figure is and will remain central in my life. On the other hand, I have to admit that the Herculean job of changing the world, even my world of the church, is practically impossible.

NOTES

[1] The office of *Reichsbischof* ("imperial bishop") was created only a few months after Hitler's coming to power in 1933 in connection with the establishment by the government of the *Reichskirche* (all-German church), an attempt to curb the power of the traditional *Landeskirchen* (regional churches). It was immediately dominated by the "German Christians", the group loyal to the new regime. One year later, the opposition led to the creation of the Confessing Church.

[2] In October 1934 the second synod of the Confessing Church instituted separate organs for the Confessing Church for administration and leadership on the local, regional and national levels. In deliberate opposition to the organs of the so-called "intact" *Landeskirchen*, and especially to counter the organs of the National Socialist *Reichskirche* and its *Führer*-ideology, they were called *Bruderräte* ("brotherly councils") rather than church- or leaders-councils.

[3] March 21, 1933, when a ceremonial service of worship was held in honour of Hitler and Hindenburg.

[4] On the night of November 9-10, 1938, the Hitler regime ordered all Jewish synagogues to be burned and demolished, Jewish shops to be looted and thousands of Jews to be arrested (later killed or put into concentration camps). Allegedly this was in reprisal for the murder of a member of the German Embassy in Paris by a Jew. The name *Reichskristallnacht* refers to the popularly held view of that time that the *Reich* had destroyed on that night all the precious glass owned by Jews. See also Chapter 5.

[5] The *Unterwegskreis* was formed during the first year after the second world war by pastors and theologians who, like Bonhoeffer, had been banned from exercising their profession. Among them were, besides Bethge, R. Wäckeling, W.D. Zimmermann and E. Lange. They were joined by G. Casalis, who was French military chaplain in Berlin. The group was important in keeping alive during the post-war years the debate of the issues arising from the experience of the Confessing Church, especially by publishing in its journal the first unpublished writings by Bonhoeffer.

[6] The *Deutsche Evangelische Kirchentag* (German Protestant Church Assembly) dates back to 1949. Held at first annually and later biennially, it emphasizes ecumenicity and lay participation in the church, gathering each time over 100,000 participants, many of them young people. It represents one of the post-war initiatives in Germany to preserve the momentum for renewal developed during the struggle of the Confessing Church.

Chapter 2

Between Confession and Resistance

Experiences in the Old Prussian Union [1]

Status confessionis in Wittenberg, 1934

On October 29, 1934, fifteen of the twenty students from the Saxony province who were studying for the ministry at the seminary in the St Augustine monastery in Wittenberg found ourselves on the street. We had been expelled on orders of the authorities of the *Reichskirche*, which had recently re-opened the seminary. For a few days we had tried to persuade the director to place the seminary under the authority of the *Bruderräte* of the Confessing Church, following the decision of the second Confessing Synod of Dahlem to separate from the *Reichskirche*. The following letter had gone to the *Reichsbischof*:

> We the undersigned would hereby like to inform you that we are in agreement with the declaration of the Confessing Synod of the German Evangelical Church of October 20, 1934. Based on this declaration we can no longer consider ourselves bound by the "conditions for participating in the curriculum of the seminary". We look to the *Bruderrat* of the Confessing Church for directions as to our future ministry.
>
> *Signed by: the 15 members of the brotherhood of auxiliary and assistant pastors in the Confessing Church studying at the Wittenberg Seminary*

Already the next morning a telegram had arrived from the *Reichsbischof* in Berlin, ordering us to leave the premises

Presented at the Congress of the Historical Commission, Berlin, 1984; a revised version was presented at the International Symposium "A Half Century after Barmen: Totalitarianism and Human Freedom in the Modern World", University of Washington, Seattle, 1984.

and, in case of refusal, threatening legal action for breach of peace.

Such was our first experience with an act of confession. Six months earlier the Confessing Synod in Barmen had declared as heretical ("we confess... we reject") the activities of the "German-Christian" church leaders, thereby introducing a *status confessionis*. Initially, the declaration was an appeal for legitimate church leadership. But the Synod soon called for the implementation of its decisions and began to take emergency measures to install its own leadership and ensure its own financial support and ministerial training.

On that 29th of October we took the call literally — and there we were, for the first time excluded from the church structure, including notably its financial support, and often from manses and even church buildings as well. For the first time the (relatively young) men in the *Bruderräte* felt the unaccustomed burden of worrying about the unemployed "illegals", the "younger brethren", especially after the Reich ministry for church affairs issued an order prohibiting the *Bruderräte* from conducting examinations, ordinations and installations. Thus the provincial *Bruderrat* of Saxony included the following warning in its convocation for the oral examination of February 29, 1936: "We shall hold the examinations... We do not want to hide the fact that we cannot give any assurance that you will be employed, receive a salary or be recognized by any office. You may well face a difficult future..."

Yet at the time our mood in Wittenberg was excellent. Finally we were free from the ambiguities of the previous six months when we had still been subject to the "German-Christian" bishops and authorities, even though they had been declared heretical by the Barmen Synod. Moreover, it soon became clear that our exodus in Wittenberg radiated encouragement to the Confessing parishes in the province. The news spread throughout Prussia and was even carried in Swiss and English newspapers.

But above all, this change in our life instilled a special intensity into our theology, our preaching, our prayers, our community life and even our singing. Just as today we may fervently sing, "We shall overcome", then we sang: *"Erhalt uns, Herr, bei deinem Wort / und steure deiner Feinde Mord, / die Jesum Christum, deinen Sohn / wollen stürzen von deinem Thron."* In the back of our mind was a (per)version of Luther's words that had been circulated by the rowdy German-Christian Bishop Hossenfelder: *"Erhalt uns, Herr, bei deinem Wort / und steure jener Frommen Mord, / die Jesum, Mensch und Gott zugleich / wollen trennen vom Dritten Reich."*[2] In a letter to his family my cousin Gerhard Vibrans wrote that "the *Reichsbischof* faces an insurmountable wall of prayer".

But we were also filled with a certain amount of pride, thinking that we had passed a rather tempting test. Our director in Wittenberg, Professor Hage, was a well-educated theologian, hardly a convinced National Socialist. As a text for our course he had chosen Emil Brunner's *Nature and Grace*. It was, to say the least, a clever choice, given Brunner's argument in favour of a theology of nature and history, and against the threatening Christomonism supposedly issuing from the writings of Karl Barth and the first thesis of the Barmen Declaration. Did this pamphlet not provide a solid theology which balanced nature and history on one side with Christ on the other as sources of revelation?

As far as I know, none of the 15 students had studied under Barth himself; nevertheless, we were already sensitized to the great temptation to which the church was exposed in these months of the Nazification of its leadership and teaching — the temptation to reach eagerly for an alibi in the form of a respected theologian and his serious theology of history. After the Hellenization of the Christian faith, why could there not as legitimately be a Germanization of it? Many went for it at the time, from the neutrals all the way to the "German Christians", from our mild seminary director all the way to a blunt NS-theology, NS-ecclesiology, NS-Christology and even NS-ethics, which had room among the *adiaphora* — the things which do not affect the truth of the gospel — for the famous "Aryan paragraph".[3]

Perhaps they thought that the study of a book by the famous Emil Brunner would lead us to take at least a neutral attitude towards the Nazification of the church and its message. But every one of us knew that after the seminaries were closed as places of insubordination the *Reichsbischof* re-opened them with the content of the curriculum and the militarized daily schedule placed under his explicit supervision.

I still have my copy of Brunner's pamphlet from those days, and I am surprised today to see where I put question marks and exclamation points then, next to passages which do not sound unreasonable today. Before leaving Wittenberg all of us, like a bunch of conspiring schoolchildren, signed our names in each other's copy and pasted in the back a copy of the letter to the *Reichsbischof* in which we had revoked our allegiance — all this to demonstrate that the time of endless debates about possible theologies of history was over, and that any statement on our situation in the Old Prussian Union, however serious and interesting, would have to be examined solely with a view to the veiled Nazification of church life and the *status confessionis*. This totally forgotten term of the Reformation, coined by Flacuis Illyricus, the Niemöller of the sixteenth century, and incorporated into the Formula of Concord, had suddenly become a keyword of our experience of fundamental change, for the fifteen of us in Wittenberg and for at least a thousand more in the Confessing Church of the Old Prussian Union. The ancient word "heresy" had been rediscovered, as if it were a new continent.

Confession — not resistance

We considered our decision and action of October 1934 exclusively as an act of confession. We were refusing the "Aryanization" of our membership of the body of Christ — that was all. None of us who was thrown out of the seminary because of this thought of political resistance. In this we were no doubt in agreement with the often-stated view of the participants in the Synods of Barmen and Dahlem.

Today it is easy to recognize the incongruity of our position. Any serious examination of the Barmen Declaration must conclude that its theses were incompatible with National Socialism and its subtle or not-so-subtle intrusions into the church. Obviously, these declarations and our local act in Wittenberg signified a limitation of totalitarian power and ideology. The Nazis were quicker to understand this than most of the people in the Confessing Church.

But at that time we refused to accept a political interpretation of our words and deeds. When the *Times* and the *Basler Nachrichten* reported our action as a sign of resistance, we reacted with anger and scorn: These people don't understand anything! They can't see that this has nothing to do with an attempt to damage, much less overthrow, the Hitler regime but serves solely the interest of blocking the Nazification of the church and renewing the church's teaching, faith and life. Most of all, such interpretations seemed to us to cloud over the source of our decision for Barmen and our readiness to take risks following Dahlem. The Lutheran theologian H. Asmussen had made a special point at Barmen that confessing *solus Christus* had nothing to do with opposition against the new Germany and its changed form of government. And even people like Karl Barth and later Dietrich Bonhoeffer expressed their low opinion of the capacity of Western theologians and editors to understand the Christ-centred tenor of the Barmen theses against the Nazification of the church. They regretted that the foreign press promoted the theses in a way that could lead to a confusion of the Confessing Church with a political resistance movement, as if it were not clear that the theses were speaking only against the Nazified pulpit (Thesis 1), the Nazified Christian life (Thesis 2), a Nazified ecclesiology (Thesis 3) and Nazified church offices (Thesis 4).

We did not interpret our decision as a choice between Christ and Hitler, between the cross and the swastika, and certainly not as a decision between democracy and a totalitarian regime. Rather, we understood the issue as one between a biblical Christ and a Teutonic-heroic Christ, between the cross of the gospels and one deformed by the swastika, as a decision in favour of the then-current slogan "Let the church be the church". We had no doubt about the front on which we had to do battle and who our real enemies were: the theological teachers, new bishops and church administrative officers who confused their enthusiasm for Hitler with Christian commitment and who thought that Christ had special regard for Germans and would preserve the racial purity of their churches. Faith and not politics, confession and not resistance, was at the root of our understanding of *status confessionis* which gave us the courage to take risks. Getting diverted into political issues could only weaken our confession of the one Christ — of that we were certain for quite some time.

As young Lutherans in 1934 we were totally unprepared for something like political resistance. We had neither experience with nor conceptions of such activities. And frankly, most of us still believed during Hitler's first years that his efforts and goals were in the best interests of Germany. When this belief began to be shaken, nobody spoke of resistance, even less so when some conscious acts of resistance were in fact committed. For by now the word had to be avoided, until after 1945. Emmi Bonhoeffer, the widow of Klaus Bonhoeffer, has recently said:

> I heard the term "resistance movement" for the first time in 1947 in Switzerland... when I visited my sister in Zurich. My brother-in-law said to me: "I suppose life is a little easier for you than for others, because your husband died in the resistance movement." "In what?", I asked. "In the resistance; that's what we call it here." I swallowed and said, "I suppose one can call it that." Why did I not know the term? It had never been used among us.

Thus in 1934 nobody stated clearly that the Barmen Confession and its enactment through the decisions in Dahlem might already involve a certain amount of blindness and delusion, of omissions and short circuits, and lead to deep confusions. In our eyes the Barmen Declaration contained no instructions for political resistance — at least not at the time. But were we really that sure?

Timid foreboding

The year 1934, the year of Barmen and Dahlem, saw certain tremors on the political scene that had to be noticed even outside the metropolis. Hitler had his former friend Ernst Röhm assassinated, as well as an unknown number of other political figures.[4] The Nazis tried to destabilize Austria by allowing the murder of Chancellor Dollfuss. After Hindenburg's death, which affected people like us, Hitler combined the functions of the chancellor and president into that of the *Führer* of all Germans. And finally, the arrest of the Lutheran bishops of Munich and Stuttgart had caused reactions in the world press. During those days my cousin wrote to his parents:

> The Third Reich is now experiencing its first serious crisis. This is not the place to raise the whole question of justice and righteousness, of truth and veracity in the Third Reich. Sin is the people's ruin, but justice elevates a people.

Suddenly there were hints that our acts of confession might touch on other dimensions. At first we noted only vague hints, which we thought it best to put out of our mind. But a certain uneasiness persisted: that with the step into the *status confessionis* the "whole question of justice and righteousness... in the Third Reich" could at one point be directed against us, the confessing Christians, the church, the public.

Against us? Wasn't it more than enough to have to cope with the experience of having left behind us the certainties of an orderly career? To explain this adventure to our worried mothers and fiancées already took some doing. And now this totally other dimension — was that not an step into an utterly new territory?

Already the first step into the reality of the *status confessionis*, with the resulting worries about employment, financial support, ministerial training and ordination, had absorbed all our energy. How would the *Bruderräte* develop and maintain all these new structures? In this area at least, we were equipped with and motivated by theological certainty. But the other area, that of "justice and righteousness", was new territory, because "Let the church be the church" had been convincingly impressed on us, and none of our leaders, including Niemöller and Barth, had said anything in public about political co-responsibility that might involve changing the political system. Who at that time, in the face of the pogroms against the Jews, dared to appeal to our political co-responsibility?

It was new territory because the traditional separation between the affairs of the state — including this National Socialist State — and the church no longer held up. This was not what we had been taught in Halle-Wittenberg.

It was also new ground because we were now obliged to seek reliable information, beyond what our controlled provincial press reported, about pogroms, the so-called Röhm-*putsch* and even the Dahlem Synod, of which we learned the details only after one of us got hold of a copy of the *Basler Nachrichten*. None of us had a radio, and the habit of listening to the BBC news from Great Britain came only much later.

It was new ground, finally, because we would eventually have to admit that Germany's "rebirth" in 1933 had been a monstrous delusion. Today, when we come across sources containing such hints, letters with more or less concealed calls, it is the result of careful research. Of course, such material can be found in the posthumous works of the Prague emigrants[5] which were smuggled into Germany under false titles and covers; but this was not material addressed to ministerial candidates, pious parishioners or pastors without any democratic tradition or experience in working in the underground. We find it now in exhibits here and there, but its effect and extent are probably overestimated.

But our hesitations in 1934 might explain our excitement a few years later when we discovered that Barth had made our question of justice the focus of his 1938 pamphlet on *Justice and Justification*. But note: only in 1938, and published only in Switzerland and accessible to us only after 1945. In 1934 we heard no such voice. Bonhoeffer was among the few who were in a position to read the 1938 text immediately. He realized that what was said here had not been expressed in this way at Barmen, and as he said to Reinhold Niebuhr at the time, "if... one states an original position in many big volumes, one ought to define the change in one's position in an equally impressive volume and not in a little pamphlet".[6]

This pamphlet, Barth's much-discussed letter to J. Hromádka and his address in Wipkingen on December 5, 1938, while in continuity with the Barmen Declaration as he had intended and prepared it, nevertheless represent new positions to which he advanced, and in which he was followed by only a few in the Confessing Church.[7]

In 1934 nobody heard that kind of thing coming either from Bonn (where Barth was teaching), Barmen or Dahlem. Bonhoeffer's voice was being heard by only a few of his former students in the embattled Berlin, later our colleagues in Finkenwalde. None of them was eager to bring to our attention Bonhoeffer's essay of 1933 on "The Church and the Jewish Question".

Nevertheless, the formulation of the confession and the acts of confessing in terms of the *status confessionis*, involving drastic changes for our theological, ecclesiastical and personal life-style, prepared the ground in which new insights could grow and new decisions be taken.

A journey into new territory

Half a year after walking out of the patrician rooms of the Augustinian monastery in Wittenberg, we found ourselves in unheatable thatched-roof huts on the Baltic Sea. The *Bruderräte* had actually succeeded in establishing five emergency seminaries in Old Prussia, among them this one (Zingst, later Finkenwalde), with its young director Dietrich Bonhoeffer, who had just returned to Berlin from a pastorate in the German parish in London. He quickly made us understand that top-level declarations against the Nazification of doctrine and practice, no matter how breathtaking, were not enough and that much remained to be done.

Already in June 1935 a new aspect could not be overlooked. The third Confessing Synod in Augsburg, whose deliberations we followed with intense interest, displayed splits between groups that had still appeared united at Barmen and Dahlem. To our consternation the Lutherans had succeeded in keeping Barth, who had moved from Bonn to Basel, away from the Synod. Nevertheless, we expected that Augsburg would affirm our acts of opposition after the decisions at Dahlem, which to our great relief it did.

But Bonhoeffer was not satisfied with the results. He had expected something else. He thought it was time that something be said about the Jews. He had inside knowledge of the preparations being made in the Ministries of Justice (where his brother-in-law Hans von Dohnanyi worked) and of the Interior for issuing the Nuremberg laws;[8] of the painful discussions going on there about who should and should not be counted as a Jew, whether the line should be drawn by one, two or three grandparents. Bonhoeffer was concerned that a protest be raised early enough to help those jurists who had scruples, as well as the future victims.

Nothing of the kind happened, of course, at Augsburg; and under the circumstances it could not have been expected. But Bonhoeffer's expectations, disappointment and his first comments opened up new perspectives for us. Gerhard Vibrans wrote in a letter to his friends that here in the Finkenwalde seminary he had met for the first time three friends of Bonhoeffer (Franz Hildebrandt, Ernst Gordon, Willi Süssbach) who had been affected by anti-Semitism, removed from their parish posts and beaten by the SA. Now they were asking Bonhoeffer for advice about emigrating. He was shaken by this face-to-face contact with the problem. To be sure, since 1933 all of us had battled against the introduction of the Aryan paragraph in the church, against the attempts to bring the churches in line with Nazi ideology, following the effective groundwork laid by Niemöller and Barth. But we had not heard of Bonhoeffer's essay on the church and the Jewish question, in which he went beyond the problem of "Jewish Christians" to discuss the task of the church to speak and eventually to act in favour of discriminated Jews ("to halt the wheel by grabbing the spokes"). The essay had hardly become known and had soon been forgotten. But now we learned for the first time what he meant and understood how isolated his stand still was.

It also became clear to us for the first time that while our Confessing Synods had developed an excellent language to speak *against* Nazification, they had no language to speak *for* its victims. Bonhoeffer kept eagerly waiting for something to be said in this regard, for neither the Barmen Declaration nor its successors contained anything.

But a word "in favour of" also derives necessarily from our belief in Christ, and it inevitably involves the act of caring for the condition of the victim, an obligation that may eventually force one to accept political involvement. Barth's pointed words in his Wipkingen address about the political commitment of a Confessing Church came out of his passionate reaction against the *Reichskristallnacht*. From now on this was the burning issue. Barmen alone would not suffice.

Bonhoeffer introduced us in 1935 to the problem of what we today call political resistance. The levels of confession and of resistance could no longer be kept neatly apart. The escalating persecution of the Jews generated an increasingly intolerable situation, especially for Bonhoeffer himself. We now realized that mere confession, no matter how courageous, inescapably meant complicity with the murderers, even though there would always be new acts of refusing to be co-opted and even though we would preach "Christ alone" Sunday after Sunday. During the whole time the Nazi state never considered it necessary to prohibit such preaching. Why should it?

Thus we were approaching the borderline between confession and resistance; and if we did not cross this border, our confession was going to be no better than cooperation with the criminals. And so it became clear where the problem lay for the Confessing Church: We were resisting by way of confession, but we were not confessing by way of resistance.

Once the border is crossed into political resistance, however, the variety and especially the ambiguity of activities to be engaged in becomes obvious. Bonhoeffer too needed some time before he became involved in the conspiracy which has become known under the date of July 20, 1944.[9] Others took even longer to reach and cross the border; and most never crossed it at all.

Today, Christians all over the world know that a *status confessionis* becomes rotten if it is limited to a confession *against* and does not go on to a confession *for*; that is to say, if the confessing Christian does not assume responsibility for society and its victims — in other words, if it is not confession *and* resistance, confession accompanied by resistance.

This is not the place to draw up the whole catalogue of possibilities of resistance,[10] or to discuss their possible applications. There were some timid initiatives in the Confessing Church, such as the *Denkschrift an Hitler* of 1936,[11] or Bishop Wurm's letters to officials during the war. The most radical form was participation in the conspiracy and the *putsch*. Experience has shown that only in the midst of the involvement can one tell which of the many levels is appropriate. Resistance can have many faces; it can be engaged in under normal, tense or extraordinary conditions. The time factor has to be considered, as do the ripeness for an action and whether the initiative should be taken by an individual Christian, perhaps in public office, or the institutional church. When Bishop Berggrav issued his interdict for the Church of Norway under German occupation, it was quite effective and politically significant, and his call for refusal to conduct funerals created a furor.

The church has a number of different options within the realm of resistance, from political opposition to an outright refusal to assume its mandate. Even the prayer of intercession cannot simply be taken for granted; it will do justice to the situation only if one has gathered the relevant information, analyzed the situation and entered into solidarity with those concerned. If not, prayer becomes a verbal exercise in creating an alibi. The church can and must make use of its possibilities to analyze the degrees of anti-Semitism and apartheid, the violations of humanity in capitalist or socialist systems, the justification for the use of means of mass destruction or of biotechnology; and it must find ways and means to oppose them.

The travels of Pope John Paul II and their political-spiritual effectiveness may have something to teach us on this point. The possibility of taking sides at a given moment must remain open, and even the risk of controlled measures of counter-violence may have to be considered, as Bonhoeffer did. The church also has a responsibility to care for the victims of a society that simultaneously produces "too much" and "too little", as well as for the victimizers. This may start with information campaigns and end up in the recognition and support of liberation movements.

People often seek a solution by assigning political action to the individual Christian and confession to the church. Obviously, there are different mandates, primary for some and secondary for others, and they are not simply interchangeable. But total separation would be dangerous, and cannot be maintained under any circumstances. For the church may be in danger of becoming abstract and docetic; and, as history has shown time and again, it may end up as an accomplice of reckless power. And the individual Christian, left alone, will be exposed to many practical and spiritual perils.

Confession and resistance

We have pointed to the lack of sensitivity to political resistance on the part of those of us who, following the Barmen Declaration, entered the *status confessionis*. We have discovered the reason for this failure in our theological tradition and in an inadequate discernment of the wider realities beyond the realm of the church. We have touched on the difficulties connected with the long path from confession to resistance, an infinitely costly way for one who embarks on it — so costly that even today the churches identify with him only half-heartedly.

By no means is it my intention to obscure, much less deny, the centrality of the act of confession, which is and remains the first and the last concern, because it means confessing Christ who brings God near to us, who directs our thoughts and hearts *against* the false gods and at the same time *towards* their victims. Resistance is connected with political calculation, rational assessment of success and appropriate strategy and tactics. It requires patience and secrecy before the blow can be risked.

Confession cannot worry about success or failure. It lives only by him whom it confesses, the crucified and risen one. Confession is a public matter. It spells out openly the name of Christ and publicly refuses praise for any other kind of messiah, whether of Teutonic, Eastern or Western origin. It is wary of any co-optation of the church; for the desire of society and the powers to co-opt the churches for their own purposes is never absent, however subtly or not so subtly this may manifest itself. Confession seeks the pulpit and if necessary the courtroom, not in order to make a show, but to give a clear and unambiguous message. Note, for instance, how Helmuth von Moltke in his last letters moved from the level of resistance to that of confessing before Judge Freisler. [12]

Resistance knows of various levels of concealment and deception requiring discipline and a sense of responsibility. It has to put up with the ambiguity of actions and actors. There is no justification prior to the action, although churches and Christians are used to it and are always eagerly looking for it.

The point at which the confession which refuses co-optation is joined by the perception of the persecuted represents the threshold of political resistance. Once the confessing Christian passes this threshold, the confession does not simply disappear, although for quite a while it may hardly be heard. It is neither simply eliminated nor totally identified with resistance. It remains alive, however hidden, with him whom it confesses. And this is of special importance in the moment of the failure of resistance, of defeat and discouragement or of the necessary healing of that which resistance had to destroy or wound.

People today who confine themselves to confession and never cross the threshold often ask how a man like Bonhoeffer could theologically justify his identification with the conspirators. The question is frightful, because it is usually raised out of an isolated and isolating situation of detached confessionalism, unconscious of its own complicity with evil. My wife once gave the shortest answer: How can a confessing Christian theologically justify a *lack of action?*

Drawing on my own experience and reflections, I would offer two conclusions:

1. Confession and resistance are not and must not become identical, neither for the sake of Christ and the church, nor for the sake of the confessing and resisting Christians, nor for the sake of the respective societies and their victims. Any monism which dissolves one into the other leads to self-destruction.

2. On the other hand, the fear that those who confess and those who resist might come too close to each other must not predominate. We are witnesses today of the cost of such fear: over

five million Jews murdered, not to speak of the survivors of the Holocaust. The Barmen Declaration did not prevent the situation which made the Stuttgart Declaration necessary. Between Barmen and Stuttgart the nameless millions lie buried. By leaving out the steps from confession to resistance, one ends up tolerating crimes, turning confession into an alibi and, in view of the injustice committed, an indictment of the confessors.

NOTES

[1] This was the name of the church that covered the territory of former Prussia. The term "union" refers to the fact that in 1817 Frederick III, King of Prussia, ordered the Lutheran and Reformed churches on his territory to be united. Curiously, the union has never been provided with a theological basis. Following World War II the name was changed to the *Evangelische Kirche der Union* (Evangelical Church of the Union).

[2] Luther's version: "Keep us within thy word, O Lord, / and do deflect the enemies' sword / who want to throw from his heavenly throne / Jesus Christ, thine only son". Bishop Hossenfelder's version: "Keep us within thy word, O Lord, / protect us against that pious horde / who wants to separate from the Reich / Jesus, man and God alike".

[3] National Socialism declared Germans as members of a superior Northern European race — the Northern "Aryans", supposedly highly endowed with biological and other human qualities. In contrast, the Jews were assigned to an inferior race which was to be eliminated. One of the first laws passed after Hitler's coming to power in 1933 ruled that no Jews were to be allowed to exercise a profession; that they were to be specifically excluded from civil service (which in Germany includes teachers and pastors). Every German was required to furnish "Aryan proof", i.e. an official certificate that neither he or she nor his or her ancestors were of Jewish origin. Church offices became involved in this process, since their registers, reaching back to the Middle Ages, enabled them to establish such certificates. The "Aryan paragraph" was initially also enforced in the churches. Dietrich Bonhoeffer was one of the few who opposed it from the beginning.

[4] Ernst Röhm was the organizer of the *Sturm Abteilung* (SA), a para-military vigilante group that was instrumental in helping Hitler to come to power. Röhm was arrested in 1934 under the pretext of having planned a *putsch* (coup) against Hitler.

[5] Following Hitler's coming to power in 1933, many of the outspoken anti-fascists, especially those from the political Left, had to fear for their safety. Prague provided a haven for many of them, at least as a first stop, though not after 1939 when the city was occupied by the Nazis (in violation of the Munich treaty signed by Hitler six months before).

6 R. Niebuhr, in *Christianity and Crisis*, Vol. V, no. 11, 1945-46, p.6.

7 In his letter to J. Hromádka (see also Ch. V, p.68) and in his address in Wipkingen (near Zurich) Barth advanced the view that political (including armed) resistance was justifiable on theological grounds and hence the duty of Christians, because National Socialism presented itself as a *religion*.

8 The Nuremberg Laws were promulgated in September 1935 (probably on the occasion of one of the Nazi party congresses, traditionally held there). The laws represent the culmination of the process of "legalizing" the discrimination against Jews in Germany, a process that had started in April 1933 with the passing of the "Aryan paragraph", prohibiting Jews from exercising a profession.

9 Date of the third and final failed attempt to assassinate Hitler. The two previous attempts had occurred in March 1943 (leading to Bonhoeffer's arrest on April 5, 1943). A group planning to overthrow Hitler had been active almost from the start of the war and included persons in the military and in government offices. The assassination plan took concrete form following the various military setbacks in late 1942 (defeats in Stalingrad and El Alamein, the Allied landing in Morocco and Algeria). Bonhoeffer became part of the group (its only theologian) after a police order had banned him from exercising any public activity (preaching, teaching, etc.). His brother-in-law Hans von Dohnanyi, a member of the resistance working in the *Abwehr* (Intelligence Service), arranged for Bonhoeffer to work in his service. In this capacity Bonhoeffer travelled to Geneva and Stockholm and, using his ecumenical contacts (e.g. with Visser 't Hooft and Bishop Bell), passed on information about the resistance to the Allies.

10 Cf. P. Steinbach, "Widerstand gegen den Nationalsozialismus", in *Machtverfall und Machtergreifung*, eds R. Lill and H. Oberreuter, Munich, R. Oldenbourg Verlag, 1983, p.305.

11 In the spring of 1936 the leadership of the Confessing Church established a documentation on illegal interference in church affairs on the part of government agencies. It mentioned acts of anti-Semitism, the concentration camps and extra-legal actions by the Gestapo. A memorandum signed by ten leaders of the Confessing Church, including Martin Niemöller, was delivered to Hitler personally. No answer to this *Denkschrift* was ever received from Hitler.

12 Helmuth von Moltke was one of the most important collaborators of Admiral Canaris in the resistance against Hitler. Founder and leader of the "Keisauer Circle", one of the resistance groups devoted to nonviolent resistance, Moltke was arrested in January 1944 and defended his participation in the resistance in front of R. Freisler, presiding judge of the "People's Court". He was executed (decapitation) in January 1945 in the Plötzensee prison.

Chapter 3

Plötzensee

Abode of Horror — Place of Redemption

While she was still speaking, the young man said, "What are you waiting for? I will not obey the king's command, but I obey the command of the law that was given to our fathers through Moses. But you, who have contrived all sorts of evil against the Hebrews, will certainly not escape the hands of God. For we are suffering because of our own sins. And if our living Lord is angry for a little while, to rebuke and discipline us, he will again be reconciled with his own servants. But you, unholy wretch, you most defiled of all men, do not be elated in vain and puffed up by uncertain hopes, when you raise your hand against the children of heaven. You have not escaped the judgment of the almighty, all-seeing God. For our brothers after enduring a brief suffering have drunk of everflowing life under God's covenant; but you, by the judgment of God, will

---

Sermon delivered during the Plötzensee memorial service, Berlin, 1994. Plötzensee, located on the *Huttigpfad* (named after Huttig, a Communist executed in 1934), is Berlin's oldest penitentiary (1872), today used as a juvenile prison. Until 1945 it was, together with the Brandenburg penitentiary, the largest execution site in northern Germany. Between 1933 and 1945, 2500 inmates from 19 nations were executed there, among them many political prisoners. Executions were either by guillotine or by rope (especially after the failed attempt on Hitler's life of July 20, 1944, with the need for mass executions). The author knew the prison from the inside, since he regularly went there to visit his friend and colleague Hans Lokies, who was in preventive detention from May to December 1941. The prison is built around a church as its centre. The inmates' cells surround the church on three sides. On the fourth side is a wall through which a door leads to the court where the executions took place. The ringing of the church bell accompanied the victims on their way. Many members of the resistance were executed in Plötzensee, especially those who had participated in the plot of July 20, 1944. On Hitler's orders they were hanged in the execution court.

receive just punishment for your arrogance. I, like my brothers, give up body and life for the laws of our fathers, appealing to God to show mercy soon to our nation and by afflictions and plagues to make you confess that he alone is God, and through me and my brothers to bring to an end the wrath of the Almighty which has justly fallen on our whole nation."

The king fell into a rage and handled him worse than the others, being exasperated at his scorn. So he died in his integrity putting his whole trust in the Lord.

Last of all, the mother died, after her sons.

2 Maccabees 7:30-41

For almost five decades we as Catholic and Protestant families of those killed in the resistance have conducted worship services on July 20 at this heavy-laden place. We do this each in our own tradition and are reverently present as brothers and sisters at each other's services. Partly we are saddened by our division; partly we are strengthened by each other's patience. Today we do it for the first time in the presence of both of our bishops.

In doing do, we are continuing what Father Odilo Braun, the deceased Dominican father, began in 1944-1945 in the prison cells at Lehrterstrasse 3. He and I supported each other in it back then. For a while I was a prisoner who did chores for the other prisoners. I gave him some wine from the bottle I found when I was cleaning up Ernst von Harnack's cell the day he was executed. He gave me some of his wafers. I brought the consecrated host in an envelope to his faithful when I carried around coffee to the cells. When the guards were not looking, I myself slipped into the cells of Friedrich-Justus Perels, Theodor Steltzer, Hermann Lindemann and others to conduct Protestant communion services.

You will understand with what emotion and joy I respond once more to the request to officiate here. But I can do that only remembering Odilo intensely and with gratitude.

What should be said after fifty years?

What should be said from a temporary pulpit beside this eerie execution site? A place where even now some of our relatives cannot bring themselves to come to sing and pray. A place where again and again new names take hold of us out of the many who were extinguished back then. In the last year, for example, I have been shaken by the story of Cato Bontjes van Beek from Fischerhude, a girl in the Red Orchestra who was decapitated here in August 1943, done away with by the same prosecutor who sent members of our families to the gallows.

But it is not the horror of Plötzensee which occupies my thoughts at this service for the fiftieth anniversary. Rather it is the proud gift which Plötzensee means for us: the gallows of Plötzensee, as did many other gallows, gave back to our family members their integrity. Now it represents our most valuable legacy. The hangmen, and above them those responsible for the murder of our families, had no idea (or maybe they did have an idea!) that with the act of execution they were in fact permanently restoring the much-injured integrity of their victims. And they did so as Germany and our churches were engulfed in the disgrace that affects all of us even now. Therefore, this memorial service must become a service of thanksgiving for an incomparable gift, the gift of martyrs, and it must bring us to participate in their world of integrity.

This was what happened. After our family members had had to exist as accomplices to the murderers during the long and tortuous years of the conspiracy, the failure of their action for humanity, for the scorned and for their rights, tore them publicly from the side of the devil to the side of God. At the moment of execution, the victim becomes stronger than the tyrant. The Maccabee son in Jewish history was right: through the martyr even the strongest tyrant brings his own demise on himself.

To be sure, for centuries we Protestants in particular have forgotten how to relate to martyrs. Still, the Reformation affirmed that the saints and martyrs should be remembered with the apostles and the prophets and given threefold honour: (1) thanks should be rendered to God for these examples of grace; (2) their example should strengthen the faith of others; and (3) others should follow their example in faith, life and steadfastness.

As late as the seventeenth century, Johann Meyfart wrote in his ardent hymn about heaven, "Jerusalem, Thou City Built High": "great prophets and Christians..., who long ago bore the yoke of the cross and suffering at the hands of tyrants, basking in honour..."[1] But soon a deficit about martyrs became evident in our sermons and hymns, our teaching and theological concepts.

A century ago Michael Baumgarten, a professor from Rostock who was demoted because he preferred rebellion for the sake of humanity to a state church which approved the *status quo*, wrote:

There are times when speeches and writings no longer adequately express the necessary truth. In such times the deeds and sufferings of the saints have to create a new alphabet, in order to reveal anew the secret of truth (1891).

Yes, "a new alphabet" of "deeds and sufferings". Plötzensee created new letters. Our worship services here year after year have worked at deciphering them.

Forty years later, Dietrich Bonhoeffer went even further in a sermon at the Kaiser-Wilhelm-Gedächtniskirche in Berlin. He added a decisive element through which alone the new alphabet of deeds and suffering can lead to the integrity of these martyrs: their entanglement in guilt. He spoke of it prophetically, not yet knowing the true form and pain it would take:

> We should not be surprised to see times approaching when martyrs' blood will be required. But this blood, should we really still have the courage and fidelity to spill it, will not be as innocent and glorious as that of the first witnesses. Our own great guilt would be part of our blood, the guilt of the unprofitable servant who is thrown into the darkness.[2]

Their and our history of guilt belongs inseparably to the new alphabet, individually and corporately; and no historical correlation can alleviate it.

This is also the point where the Auschwitz martyrdom of the Jews demands a different alphabet from ours here today!

By what measure do we honour here our martyrs and let them set examples?

We honour examples like Paul Schneider — for us Protestants — and Joseph Metzger — for you Catholics — in their obedience to God, as pure as that of the classic Maccabee sons before the tyrant Antiochus. We take no offence against them.

But how do our relatives from the conspiracy convince us that they are models for us in God's name? To do so, it helps to take seriously the old classic criteria. And faith, in order to remain faith, has to acknowledge the entanglements of this century of German history.

Four attributes characterize the martyrs of Plötzensee:

1) the free affirmation of a deed whose risks are suffering and martyrdom;

2) the rejection of martyrdom that is longed for or pathologically chosen;

These first two criteria come from early Christian times, and they open the way for including these names in liturgy and religious instruction.

3) the measure of solidarity with guilt and acceptance of guilt; with this we really mean our own families in the midst of the reality of resistance;
4) the authentically Christian nature of the martyrdom of our relatives, difficult to measure: martyrdom "for Christ's sake".

1. First, death in Plötzensee witnesses to life because of its free acceptance of a deadly deed for the sake of that humanity which for years was being destroyed in Germany. There are deaths which witness only to death: Auschwitz, Sarajevo, Kigali leave behind only silence and devastating accusations. But there are also deaths which witness to life: the Scholls' of the "White Rose", Father Alfred Delp's, Count von Moltke's, Cato Bontjes van Beek's. Even in tribulation and weakness they send out signals of consolation, even now. Responsibility was freely accepted; blood sacrifice was elevated to a message which could create faith. Of course, free acceptance did include the vexing question: must it be I who has to step out of the ranks? But it is the free "Yes" to the deed with its risk which casts their deaths in Plötzensee as martyrdom and witness.

2. Confronted with a trend of overwhelming longing for martyrdom, the early Christians decided that enthusiastic, self-chosen martyrdom was without the promise. I think that this distinction clarifies elements of the martyrdom of Plötzensee in a comforting way.

We do not dispute that in all ages there have been joyous sacrifices for ideas and idols. Even for Hitler some relatively pure souls ran directly into machine guns to sacrifice themselves for the one who claimed to fulfil dreams. But the command and applause of the idol accompanied the hour of their death. They possessed the approval of the nation. In contrast, our martyrs went through the agonies of general rejection. Public contempt isolated their bodies and souls. They were to be extinguished without a grave — unappreciated, silenced, in an ambiguous death, belated failures.

This was not to be a sacrificial, heroic public act in the market square, but an end in the incognito of camps and cellars, in places of shame like Plötzensee.

3. The fact of guilt, its acceptance and their solidarity with it is the strongest distinction between the martyrdom of Plötzensee and usual images of martyrs. That stamp by gallows and scaffolds becomes what it is only in light of this aspect. Their martyrdom grew out of the guilt of the churches, who had given up being faithful to all people and had accepted being limited to their "own people". It further grew out of the guilt of politicians and officers who, bound by duty, forsook their own responsibility. The result was that entire sectors of the population were devalued and destroyed and other countries were ravaged, so that one day the best Germans had to share in the guilty history of a conspiracy. That is what created the martyr of our time: no longer a saintly pure witness, but a guilt-covered witness for humanity, no longer distant from the contemporary world, but winning back integrity only by way of fully accepting the guilt and paying the price.

4. I mention the measure "for Christ's sake" only in fourth place. Actually it should come first. Full solidarity with Christ, that is through him, in him and with him. That also means the way we will receive him later in the eucharist. But everyone will understand if I hesitate here. Everyone will understand that while on the one hand "for Christ's sake" is the strongest measure and mark of martyrdom it need not be in the forefront. Indeed, we are all aware of the possibility that it can be misused as a dogmatic imperative, aware also of the great harm caused when Christians are preoccupied with measuring the record of achievements and with worries about the proper Christian identity. The latter might even tempt us to reinterpret our own martyrs.

In fact we need to discover to our shame the extent to which humanity is the goal and truth of the Christian message. Whether the "for Christ's sake" was openly confessed or implicit at the time, we know, even apart from several cases of great final confessions of faith, that our family members deeply identified with those who were stripped of their humanity. But none of them advertised their Christian identity. And that was as it should be. Not only because Christian identity had been compromised to the core (in a long prior history), but also because deeds done lose their power by over-zealous interpretation. Self-affirmation only weakens the message of martyrs, which is strongest when it is accompanied by restraint in talking about itself. It is enough if here and there one of them intermittently spoke of solidarity "with the most defenceless and weakest brethren of Christ".[3] The gift of Christian identity must be treasured and not advertised. Even in this worship service, we do not in any way judge these martyrs; they judge and mark us.

The seal of Plötzensee
Our annual path to this unique worship service belongs to the ways in which they mark us. We are spelling out the alphabet which they spoke. Its authority is final. No changes or contradictions can be added. The church used to lift martyrs up into the ranks of the apostles and prophets, because their message of Christ's work for humanity could never be corrupted again, and because they concluded their lives with a straightforwardness which none of the living can equal.

We can no longer ask our Plötzensee relatives any questions. Nor do they need our support or justification. Our deciphering and our attempts to understand Plötzensee reach their goal in the power of shame which radiates from them thanks to the seal of this place. The power is great, creative and lasting. It is greater than that of synods or of official authorities, greater also than the authority of historians, whom we must someday find ways of reminding of their limitations, lest the results of their research take the place of the living and deadly events. No, the shame of Plötzensee is an incomparable gift to us, full of inexhaustible treasures of renewal.

Since the fourth century, the church has sung in the *Te Deum*:

God of power and might,
heaven and earth are full of your glory.
The glorious company of apostles praise you.
The noble fellowship of prophets praise you.
The dear assembly of martyrs praise you.
Throughout the world the holy church acclaims you;
Father, of majesty unbounded,
your true and only Son, worthy of all worship,
and the Holy Spirit, advocate and guide.
... Our hope is in you, dear Lord,
Bring us from shame forevermore.

NOTES

[1] "Propheten gross und Patriarchen hoch, auch Christen insgemein, die weiland dort trugen des Kreuzes Joch und der Tyrannen Pein, schau ich in Ehren schweben, in Freiheit überall, mit Klarheit hell umgeben, mit sonnenlichtem Strahl."

[2] June 19, 1932; *Gesammelte Schriften*, IV, p.71.

[3] Dietrich Bonhoeffer, *Ethics*, p.114.

Chapter 4

How the Prison Letters Survived

On July 20, 1944, the day of the failed coup against Hitler, my unit of German military intelligence was occupying a much too lovely requisitioned villa on the high ridge of San Polo d'Enza in northern Italy, near Parma, about 20 kilometres south of the Via Emilia, where the first Apennine peaks with their castle ruins overlook the small town.

I had a lot of time to sit on the sunny terrace and think about the famous ruins of Canossa, where Henry IV had done penance to Pope Gregory VII in 1077, only 10 kilometers further south. But one could not visit that area, because Italian partisans controlled every hill and valley. In one of the letters smuggled out of Tegel prison in Berlin, Dietrich Bonhoeffer had written that because of the Hitler regime we would have to think differently about Canossa.[1] We had been taught to sympathize with Henry IV, but now we came to sympathize with Pope Gregory as well: "We were taught at school that all these great disputes were a misfortune to Europe, whereas in point of fact they are the source of the intellectual freedom that has made Europe great."[2]

Only a few weeks had passed since the Allied offensive northwards, which had spared Rome, and with it the Vatican, which Dietrich had loved for more than 20 years. In my letters I now hinted that I was near Canossa.

First published in 1987 in a festschrift for the Dutch theologian and ethicist G. Th. Rothuizen, *Het leven is meer dan ethik*.

Not far from Rome

The intelligence unit to which I had belonged since January was a small unit of 16 men. It was supposed to bring intelligence from behind our lines — and whenever possible from behind the enemy front — to the headquarters of Field Marshal Albert Kesselring, commander of German forces in Italy. But we ordinary soldiers had little to do with that. We serviced the vehicles, foraged and stood night watch. The officers did the real tasks. They were the "un-Prussian" Major Tilp from Austria and the "Prussian" Lieutenant Sarstedt from Hanover (who had recently insisted on our standing guard at night and was therefore not very popular with us). In addition, there was a widely experienced sergeant from Dresden, who was soon promoted to sergeant-major. There were also a few non-commissioned officers from Bavaria, who were warm-hearted and unscrupulous at the same time, and a few skilled bilingual men from Southern Tyrol. Among them was J. Rainalter, a lawyer from Meran, who soon became my confidant. I gave him pages of Bonhoeffer's letters to read when he wasn't away on duty, for example interpreting at the offices in Milan.

At first there was no real place for me in the unit. "We didn't ask for you; what shall we do with you?" This was the commanding officer's first reaction, as I wrote in a letter home on January 24, 1944. When I was still in basic training in Lissa, Poland, a non-commissioned officer had let me look at some papers in the briefing room. As I then reported in a letter to my wife Renate, the papers said that I "should be sent to a field unit of the *Abwehr* (military intelligence). Bethge has worked for the *Abwehr* and should be kept in it because of his knowledge." To Renate I added: "Signed by Justus's man." "Justus" was Klaus Bonhoeffer's brother-in-law, Justus Delbrück, and "his man" was Count Karl-Ludwig von Guttenberg. Both had been brought by Hans von Dohnanyi to Admiral Canaris and were still working in the *Abwehr* headquarters in Berlin, where they could arrange such personal matters to help the family. Thus I was not sent to die on the Russian front but would have a better chance in Italy. By July I had been promoted two ranks to lance-corporal, and some months earlier Tilp had made me clerk of the unit.

Things has been different before the Allied offensive had started towards the northern Apennines from around Cassino and

Anzio-Nettuno. Back then our unit had lived in an isolated farmhouse among fields and olive groves on the Via Flaminia near Rignano, thirty kilometres north of Rome, beneath the cliffs of Monte Soratte. On a clear day you could make out from the mountain the spire of St Peter's dome. My father-in-law had copied out for me Horace's poem about the snow-covered Soratte.[3] Kesselring's headquarters, now situated halfway up the mountain in deep tunnels, was soon plagued with massive bombing attacks. But we still had to go there several times a week, not only for provisions, but even more for the mail — for me the most important was the mail from my wife in Berlin-Charlottenberg and from Bonhoeffer in Tegel prison.

Moreover, in February our unit had established an auxiliary base in the lovely small city of Velletri, southeast of Rome. Of course, it was less attractive for us after the English and Americans had established a beachhead at Anzio and Nettuno. Here, too, we were in a requisitioned villa much too fine for us, though it no longer had any windowpanes, since the city was within range of fire from Allied ships. When I saw our villa for the first time, red wine lay ankle-deep on the cellar floor around the casks. In those days I often had to chauffeur the major between Rignano and Velletri in one of our most modern Citroëns. Sometimes I was at the wheel, sometimes on the front fender to watch for air attacks on the road.

On these trips there were regular stops in the "Eternal City", for example when the major had to go there in connection with the shooting of hostages in the Ardeatine Caves.[4] Only after the war did I realize that this was what he was doing: we underlings were not informed and it was hardly possible for us to listen illegally to foreign radio broadcasts. Those hours in Rome were free for me and they helped a great deal to compensate for the danger of the trips to Velletri.

My hints in letters to Dietrich in his Tegel prison cell of visiting Rome in the spring had excited him. He immediately remembered our own visit to Rome in 1936 and even more his impression twelve years earlier of the Laocoön statuary in the Vatican museum.[5] He thought immediately of whom I should look up in the Vatican in case I got into a critical situation, because we had been together with several people from the Vatican in Ettal in 1940.[6] But I made it as far as a papal audience for German soldiers only once. Hundreds of us filed by Pius XII, and we were given a picture of him posing in deep prayer. I tried quickly to let him know that I was an illegal pastor of the Confessing Church, but to my disappointment he gave no sign of responding. In any case, entire passages about Rome in Dietrich's letters from Tegel are due to this chauffeur work for Major Tilp between February and May 1944.

Meanwhile, even Rignano did not remain the idyllic setting we had found at first, when Rainalter and I had taken long walks through the hills and ravines and revealed our liking for each other. The closer the Allied offensive came, the more the hissing Spitfires made daylight targets of the Flaminia and the Soratte, so that we felt safe only at night. Then the entrances to Kesselring's mountain headquarters were wreathed in clouds of dust, and I was afraid that my leave, which was already approved for my son's baptism in Berlin, would be cancelled. If so, I would lose the chance to see Dietrich, whom we intended to make a godfather, as well as Friedrich Justus Perels, who was also to become a godfather for my son as I was for his son. But in the end I was able to depart for this leave. During my long odyssey to get to the train, which could come only as far as 50 kilometres north of where I was, I just missed the beginning of the Allied offensive, which caused my unit in Rignano and Velletri to flee headlong through Rome up to Florence.

When I returned weeks later, I found our unit intact in Montevettolini, an idyllic wine village on the heights between Florence and Lucca. I was given my first military promotion, to private first class, for having succeeded in reaching my own unit despite the chaos of units being dissolved and reorganized between Munich, Verona and Florence. Today I wonder if the correspondence to and from Tegel prison could have continued if I had abruptly been put into a unit on the fighting front. Would we ever have received the letters Dietrich continued to send to the *Abwehr* unit using the old field post number? And those letters were the ones of April and May 1944 with those theologically brilliant passages.

In November 1943 Dietrich had arranged for correspondence with me to be smuggled through Knobloch, one of his guards. I took along the letters from then until May on my trip back to

Berlin, and we buried most of them in gas mask containers in Schleichers' garden. We actually found them again after the war — not something to be taken for granted, for many similar caches were not found again, or if they were found, they had already been plundered by others.

Not far from Canossa

Now in San Polo d'Enza I spent the long warm July days in our opulent villa, while the major, lieutenant and the others disappeared to do other things. I took care of the mail, and had a lot of time to myself for correspondence. At that point I began to make copies of the theological passages in Dietrich's letters on the office typewriter. I had asked Dietrich for permission. Finkenwalde friends like Albrecht Schönherr, Winfried Maechler and Wolf-Dieter Zimmermann ought to have a chance to think about the passages which were surprising and exciting me off in Italy. We young Confessing pastors were used to criticizing religion, and we included that in our sermons more or less skillfully. But this went further and deeper. Dietrich probably sensed that I could hardly keep from passing on his new thinking. This is how he described his own feelings about his new Tegel thoughts starting with his letter of April 30.

> By the way, it would be very nice if you didn't throw away my theological letters, but sent them on to Renate from time to time, as I'm sure they're too much of a burden for you. Perhaps I might want to read them again later for my work. One writes some things more freely and more vividly in a letter than in a book, and often I have better thoughts in a conversation by correspondence than by myself.[7]

I was very gratified by these sentences and by the amazing flow of thoughts which continued from week to week. I felt simultaneously proud and helpless — uplifted by his trust and at the same time in over my head. So I longed to exchange ideas not only with Rainalter, a Catholic and theologically inexperienced, but also with our Berlin friends. I probably also hoped to become more sure of myself in the replies I wrote to Dietrich's reflections. I had no idea that these pages would someday be known around the world. Today it is somewhat difficult for me to remember how I felt when the post arrived with such thoughts. I have thought and written too much about them since then, and heard and read even more! My first — and at that point only — partner in reading them, Rainalter, began to be as curious as I was to see what the next mail would bring, though he was often away.

My comrades had assignments in Reggio Emilia, in Milan or on forays in the mountains. Those reconnaissance tasks in the valleys and ravines full of partisans were undoubtedly unpleasant. There must have been ghastly atrocities there too. I did not ask much about them, or I repressed them quickly.

Once I had to be more than just the unit clerk. Our people brought along a captured civilian whose interrogations had apparently not been completed. He was an educated Italian of the same type as the owner of our villa, whom we had humiliated by confiscating his house and vandalizing his valuable chests and desks. The new prisoner was locked up in our cellar, and during the day I brought him food. Despite the language difficulties, we began to talk together. When I told him I was a Protestant pastor, he suddenly asked me to hear his confession and give him absolution. He would not be dissuaded when I explained to him that I had no authority from the Catholic Church. The parts of the confession I understood had little to do with the possible reasons for his arrest. He just wanted to be reconciled with himself in the event of a bad outcome of his case. Without my experience of individual confession and absolution in Bonhoeffer's Finkenwalde seminary, I would have been rather helpless that day. I never heard anything more about that man's whereabouts or fate.

And the twentieth of July? That evening is crystal clear in my memory. My daily tasks included presenting the army report and other dispatches at supper. The first brief report of an assassination attempt at Hitler's headquarters caused deep shock.

For even in San Polo d'Enza I was rather well informed. First, Dietrich and I had mentioned the possible date of a coup ("it can't be long now") in our one-hour conversation in a solitary cell in Tegel prison in early June. Second, in her daily letters Renate had learned to use the family's code words perfectly. In those weeks Klaus Bonhoeffer had the closest ties to the central planners of the coup, and they had expressed more and more clearly their optimism for what was coming. So even far away I hoped that we would not have to wait much longer for the changes a coup would bring.

But now the appalling dispatch had come. What was I supposed to think of it, without any possibility of asking questions or exchanging reactions? Did it really happen the way the German radio reported? Finally Major Tilp appeared at the huge antique wooden table in the dining room. He took his pistol from its holster, laid it in front of him on the table and began to remind us about "the treason against the *Führer* of 30 June 1934" and said, "If anyone utters a word against the *Führer*, I will shoot him! *Heil Hitler!*"

Was Tilp such a Nazi? Did he feel obliged at that moment, for reasons we did not know, to react in such an extreme way? My own thoughts flew to Berlin, to the Marienburger Allee 42 and 43, to Sakrow,[8] behind the walls of Tegel prison and to the prison hospital at Buch, where Hans von Dohnanyi lay paralyzed and isolated. As soon as possible, I withdrew, in order not to have to talk. Rainalter was away. Usually I went to sleep quickly, but that night I hardly slept at all until morning. If the dispatches were even close to accurate, was everything lost by the next day for the family, for their prisoners, for a different Germany? How did things really look back home? When would I hear something?

Did this mean an end to the letters? Would some of them fall into the wrong hands? The fastest field post between Berlin and San Polo d'Enza took about ten days, but it could just as easily take four weeks. Soon we noted that no "unimportant" freight had been transported across the Po river for 14 days (then I got 14 letters from Renate all at once!). How long would I have to wait for the first news about events at the Marienburger Allee or in the Tegel prison cell? An enlisted man was not allowed to use the telephone. And from the other direction, a telegram to me from Berlin was impossible: what could it say without calling attention to itself?

Actually there should still have been a number of letters from Dietrich on the way to me. Would they now be intercepted — with unthinkable consequences?

During my leave in May, Christel von Dohnanyi had urged us to stop smuggling letters between Tegel prison and Italy. I discussed this with Dietrich when I visited him in prison, but we had decided to continue. Of course we had to be careful about what we said and how we said it, but we thought we could confidently keep using our channel via the experienced and trustworthy Knobloch, which had worked so well for the previous eight months. He addressed the envelopes in his own hand and received and forwarded the letters from his home address in Frohnau.

But now? In fact, more letters from Dietrich soon arrived, but they were from the time before July 20, according to his dates and the Frohnau postmark. But at least it was something! On July 31 I wrote to Renate, "When will I know something from Tegel, Eichkamp, etc.?"[9] When Renate's first letter after July 20 arrived from Berlin, it contained not a word about changes I should follow.

Finally Dietrich's letter of July 21 also arrived.[10] Ever since then it has been my favourite. His response to that moment which was darkest for him, the devastation of all his own and our common hopes, was to think first of our situation waiting far away before setting down his own reflections and summing up his life, now surely about to end, and his questions and answers. Soon thereafter his poem "Stations on the Way to Freedom" arrived, with its final verse about death as a station. He wrote about it in his letter of July 28, the fourth written after the failed coup, arriving as always via Knobloch:

> Not only action, but also suffering is a way to freedom. In suffering, the deliverance consists in our being allowed to put the matter out of our own hands into God's hands. In this sense death is the crowning of human freedom. Whether the human deed is a matter of faith or not depends on whether we understand our suffering as an extension of our action and a completion of freedom. I think that is very important and very comforting.[11]

Today the words "very important and very comforting" tell me of his joy that it was now all out in the open: the long period of conspiracy really was the true path of liberation from the way "decent people" were sucked into complicity with evil. Thus "suffering" and "death" now belonged inseparably to the act of liberation.

Today the surviving letters show how unimpeded Dietrich's August letters were in getting to San Polo d'Enza *after* July 20. And all the things they contained: drafts of *Who am I?*, of *Christians and Pagans* and, of course, of the "Stations"... I immediately copied them by hand and sent them to my wife and thus the family in Berlin. A cousin who suddenly turned up at our villa on his way back to Germany to join a new unit took portions of the letters along, so that they could be kept there or by my mother, who lived in the village of Kade, between Brandenburg and Magdeburg. These included a photo of Dietrich Bonhoeffer in the yard of Tegel prison with papers in his hand. I wrote to Renate on August 4: "I have just received a picture of Dietrich, the Big One [in contrast to our six-month-old son]. He is in shirt sleeves, somewhat wearied by the heat, doesn't look quite himself, I think." Then I continued, "By the way, a poem came again yesterday, linguistically particularly well done, which I shall write out for you..."[12]

In spite of all that, a sense of isolation dominated my days. And there seemed to be no end to Rainalter's work in Milan. On August 7 I wrote home sarcastically, "When the names of the villainous officers [in the conspiracy] were announced yesterday, here they all said, rightly enough, 'Of course, nothing but counts and barons.' They have all become much braver and more resolute." Perhaps that response was an early form of today's dreadful schema of dividing the resistance into only two groups: the "nationalist-conservatives" and the "socialist-communists". Of course, in those days the officers were the only resisters uncovered, but even back then some of us knew better.

So our correspondence continued almost unchanged week after week. The Gestapo headquarters, the Reich Security Head Office (RSHA), had not yet found any evidence of how long and how deeply Hans von Dohnanyi, the Bonhoeffer brothers and their brothers-in-law were implicated in the complex which led to the events of July 20. At first the events themselves were the primary object of the investigation. Today we know more precisely how irrevocably that changed with the finding of the so-called Zossen Files on September 22, 1944, by RSHA-Commissar Sonderegger. Sonderegger had been present when Dietrich was arrested by Röder and at Dietrich's interrogations. It was he who had found the file cabinet in the evacuation depot of the *Abwehr*.[13] From then on, the situation deteriorated catastrophically.

To be sure, Dietrich's letters did begin to include coded suggestions, rare up to that point, of whom I could contact in case I should be taken prisoner by the Allies. In addition to ecumenical contacts, Gaetano Latmiral's name appears in this context.[14] He was an Italian officer and physics professor from Naples also imprisoned in Tegel at that time. Since then he has become close to us through the International Bonhoeffer Society. Dietrich's letters also included suggestions of how I should describe our relationship if I were swept into the maelstrom of interrogations. In his last surviving letter of August 23 he wrote:

> By the way, H[ans] and O[ster] were very interested in your missionary work; I had nothing to do with it. Nothing was said about it previously. Our connection is essentially through church music and academic theology; in addition, Renate was the great point of attraction.[15]

When I really was questioned later by the Gestapo commissars, I followed the line he suggested — with success.

For my part in San Polo d'Enza I continued to copy passages on "non-religious interpretation" — also for Renate's father, as I wrote to her on August 14 — and to send Dietrich's accumulated letters to my mother. It was especially important now that these smuggled letters not further endanger anyone.

Still, nothing changed in our correspondence, even when the first news came from Renate that Klaus Bonhoeffer was arrested on October 1 and Rüdiger Schleicher on October 4. They were in solitary confinement in the RSHA prison, Lehrterstrasse 3 in Berlin. At first her father refused to accept the food her mother brought to the prison for him and Klaus, because he did not want the family to go hungry for his sake. At that point Christel von Dohnanyi sent another warning that we should not further endanger anyone by continuing our illegal correspondence. I really did curtail my writing. But what did Dietrich want? I wrote to him on September 21:

> What will you think of me! I don't know what to do, as I've been vehemently given such conflicting advice. But perhaps it's superfluous.[16]

During those days the poem "The Death of Moses" arrived. Only much later did I find out what really happened in early October in Berlin: Dietrich's plan to escape and his forgoing it, Klaus and Rüdiger's arrests, Dietrich's transfer on October 8 from the tolerable military prison in Tegel to the harsh cellar of the RSHA prison in the Prinz-Albrecht-Strasse. From then on no further word which Dietrich had addressed to me ever reached me.

But in Italy I could not know anything about all that in October. His last directly forwarded letters from September showed signs of the darkening skies over the whole family and close friends like Perels, but they also contained continuations of his theological thought. The famous "Outline for a Book" had arrived just before the contact broke off. To be sure, there was a comment in the same letter about the false rumour that Oster had committed suicide, and it mentioned that Dietrich himself no longer kept anything with him in his cell.[17] He gave my letters to him to his parents during their visits to the prison. They gave them back to me after the war, with dates through the end of September. My first news of the new arrests on October 1 and 4 came from Renate's letter, which arrived in San Polo d'Enza relatively quickly on October 13.

During those same October days an article appeared in *New English Weekly* which for the first time had the courage to inform the British public that the people who had been involved in the plot of the 20th of July were not just another military clique intent on removing Hitler for their own selfish ends. Gerhard Leibholz was the author.[18]

Not far from Mantua

On October 18 our unit was evacuated from our luxurious villa and sent northward. We had mixed feelings about it. The Po was swollen by downpours and for everyone crossing it on the long pontoon bridges there was a further horror from the aggressive Spitfire attacks. In case of retreat, at least the Po would no longer be an obstacle between us and home. In the meantime Major Tilp had been promoted away from us and Lieutenant Sarstedt had taken his place. Corporal Weiss, against whom I had lost many games of chess, was killed by a partisan's shot.

I wrote home that they should imagine my location near the birthplace of Vergil, author of the *Aeneid* — Mantua, where the Tyrolean patriot Andreas Hofer was betrayed into the hands of Napoleon's forces and shot in 1810. I had no idea that I would hardly have time to get to know it, but there was enough time to move into an enormous, previously plundered palace, which I described in a letter to Renate as "mouse-infested". Even there I had time to type excerpts from the theological passages of Dietrich's most recent letters. Evidence of this is in a letter I wrote to Renate on October 26, two days before I hastily destroyed all suspicious papers.

That was a Saturday. In my last letter from the field, dated October 28, there is a postscript obviously written in the late evening:

> Summon all your courage now. I have just learned that I have to be taken to Berlin. But why? ... Have trust and patience... You will be able with me confidently to face everything we have to bear. You know that a man likes to clear up his case, dispel any suspicions and eliminate any threats to the general welfare. That is what Father is doing, and that is what I shall do now. Perhaps, I hope, we will even be able to help each other... In terms of the external circumstances, don't worry about me. You know that I can make my way easily and well through any situation. We will hear from each other less often, but the field post has already given us some experience at that.

This was written in a way that assumed that my letters from the field were already being censored.

What had happened on that evening? Towards six o'clock — it was already dark — our motorcycle messenger returned from the mail office in Mantua. Following orders, he gave me the official mail. In it there was a sealed envelope with a confidential telegram.

Major Tilp had long since authorized me to open such cables with the rest of the mail and to put it all on his desk. Amazingly, Sarstedt had continued this practice. So it happened that I was the very first one to read this telegram. It contained the dry order: Lance Corporal Eberhard Bethge is to be brought immediately to the Reich Security Head Office at the Kurfürstenstrasse, Berlin, under heavy guard.

My first reaction was that I should destroy the telegram. But that was impossible. It would cause trouble for my comrade, who had just signed a receipt for it in Mantua. My second reaction was to go to my locker. I was alone, no comrades in the room, no officer or sergeant next door. I collected all the letters and notes in Dietrich's handwriting — and perhaps also those excerpts — and burned them in the iron stove in the clerk's room. I have always thought that there was at least an additional month of letters, from September. Now the letter from August 23 appears to be the last, but it was not the last, as is evident in comments in letters to my wife in which I passed along nice remarks from Dietrich about me. Unfortunately, those remarks say nothing about the progress of his theological thinking. At the time in the clerk's room, I had to destroy all traces of smuggling. How could I know how my ambitious boss would react? Sarstedt might even get additional orders by telephone from Berlin and try to get a reply to the sender of the telegram at the RSHA that the order had been carried out. How could I endanger Dietrich, Knobloch and myself by keeping evidence which was perhaps not yet discovered?

My third reaction was to go out in the cool of the evening to think. There I ran into the non-commissioned officer Frank, an intelligent and tough old soldier recently awarded the Iron Cross for a reckless but surely also ghastly action against partisans in the mountain villages south of San Polo d'Enza. Sometimes he said he coveted more education, and for some time he had tried to get closer to me whenever Rainalter was away for a while. That night Rainalter was away. I told Frank about the telegram. His heated response was: "There is only one way, defect immediately to the partisans!" This was a more sober and distrustful assessment of my chances than the commanding officer was to give shortly thereafter. But I told him that this was impossible. I had an aged mother at home and a young wife with a baby. I could not endanger the family even more by deserting. In addition, I knew I was not the type of person who could take risks in the mountains controlled by the partisans and get very far. Yes, it really was impossible! In that conversation Frank, a mercenary type and survival artist, was full of spontaneous warmth. I went back in, put the mail in order, placed it on Sarstedt's desk and went up to supper. It was seven o'clock.

Soon the commander appeared there: "Now, then, Bethge, what is this thing with you?" It sounded more friendly than inquisitorial. I answered that I had heard that my father-in-law was involved in some interrogations and perhaps they needed me for them. There was also such a thing as suspects' relatives being arrested. He said: "It won't be too bad. We will attend to it tomorrow. We'll send you up to Berlin, and in two weeks you'll be back here with us. You can leave your gear here." Nothing was said about searching or confiscating anything, nothing about a telephone call to the RSHA. When after a few days I knew of all the opportunities there would have been before I was finally shut into solitary confinement, I might really have gotten upset at the thought of the letters I had just burned. But thoughts like that only came to me much later.

The next morning Sarstedt delegated two non-commissioned officers, Stahl and Rummelsberger, to accompany me. They were both no longer young, fathers of families in Bavaria, full of inner decency although they had seen a lot. Stahl had already gone with me in one difficult situation. That was during our move from Montevettolini to San Polo d'Enza when I had to drive an ancient Fiat at night across the Apennines. With no spare parts at all we finally rumbled in, driving on spokes and rims, and reported: "Mission accomplished!" And Rummelsberger was the sort who would protest when things got too ugly and cynical at meals; once he showed some interest in my pictures of my family in Berlin.

I kept on my epaulets and corporal insignia during the long journey, but I was no longer allowed to carry sidearms. The sergeant filled all my pockets with cigarettes, the irreplaceable currency in those days. We had the good luck to travel up the Brenner pass when it was overcast and rainy, and even in Munich we were spared bombing raids. First off, the two NCOs went to visit their wives there, leaving me to my own devices. I cannot remember if while in Munich I visited Dietrich's cousin Ninne Kalckreuth and the wife of Dr Josef Müller, who was also imprisoned in Berlin, as I had often done before. I did not dare to try to telephone the family in Berlin, because both houses in the Marienburger Allee were probably under surveillance.

If I remember rightly, we boarded the night train to Berlin two evenings later. In the morning, when we passed through Jüterbog in Fläming, just south of Berlin, I said to my guards, who were just waking up, "You don't need to take me to the Kurfürstenstrasse right away. If we go to the Marienburger Allee first, my mother-in-law will fix you a fine dinner." I gave them a lot of my cigarettes, and they readily agreed.

All night long I had considered how I might contact the family to let them know that I too was now a prisoner in Berlin, perhaps to be held in the same prison as Klaus and Rüdiger, and to warn Renate not to send any more letters by field post to Italy, but to bring food parcels and toiletries to the prison, and perhaps even smuggled information, just as they did for the other prisoners in the family.

Towards noon we really did arrive at Marienburger Allee. It was foggy. I looked around to see if the two houses were being guarded, but they were not. I rang the bell. The door opened, and there stood not only my mother-in-law, but also Renate, who happened to be there with little Dietrich rather than in Sakrow, where she had been staying to be a little safer from the air raids on the city.

Now everything worked out as I had hoped. To feed Stahl and Rummelsberger, Renate's mother took what she needed from her precious cache of food intended for the men in prison. Upstairs Renate and I exchanged information which I might need to know about the status of the four prisoners' interrogations. She told me that a note could be turned in at the prison gate together with food and laundry and a note could be received with a specific wish from a prisoner. This was done by bribing the guards with cigarettes. In addition, we were officially pre-trial prisoners and not convicts in a concentration camp. We agreed that, if my interrogations seemed to centre on her father, Rüdiger Schleicher, I would ask for a toothbrush. If they had more to do with Dietrich, I would ask for a facecloth.

But what could we do to let the Gestapo know that the family knew what it was not supposed to know — that I had arrived in Berlin? Renate's mother found a solution. That morning she had been at the Kurfürstenstrasse Gestapo office regarding her husband's case. Commissars Günther and Baumer had not received her, but had sent her away to return in the late afternoon. So she departed with the city train from the nearby Heerstrasse station at 4:00 pm. Stahl, Rummelsberger and I took the 4:10 pm train. And it worked out that as we entered the hall in the Gestapo office, my mother-in-law was standing there. She hurried over to me and embraced me, saying, "You here?" At the same moment Baumer came down the steps, saw us and separated us angrily. But now the RSHA knew that the family was informed about me. Already the next day Renate appeared in the Lehrterstrasse 3 with a food parcel, and learned my cell number: 235.

Lehrterstrasse 3

But it was days, even weeks, before she received a request for either a toothbrush or a facecloth. At first greetings and thanks were all she got when she delivered me warm meals wrapped in many layers of newspaper. There was no interrogation. The prison was built according to a British model of a century earlier. It was star-shaped with single cells in each wing. On the inside, we hoped that this would protect us from becoming an air raid target. Everyone knew almost everyone else in the prison, which had been cleared out for political prisoners after the 20th of July. Besides me, I knew that Rüdiger Schleicher and Klaus Bonhoeffer, Friedrich Justus Perels and Hans John (Schleicher's assistant), Justus Delbrück and Baron Guttenberg, Ernst von Harnack, Walter Bauer, Adolf Lampe, Constantin von Dietze and Gerhard Ritter, Theodor Steltzer and Kleist from Schmenzin were all there. For a while Hanns Lilje and Günther Harder were also kept there. But at first we could only make contact with glances, when doors were opened to distribute meals and we came to the doorways. We really saw each other only when we were finally permitted a short exercise in the prison yard. That was a great moment.

Finally in the second half of November I was fetched in handcuffs to the Kurfürstenstrasse office. Commissar Baumer interrogated me. A secretary wrote the transcript, but only from his dictation. I was not allowed to formulate my answers for it. I then had to sign seven copies of the transcript. From time to time, Commissar Günther would look in and ask pointedly, "Is he talking?" ... "Is he talking yet?" ... "He'll talk!" I was never physically tortured. Once I was suddenly brought down to the basement, but that frightening development turned out to be because of an air raid. Questions about my mother, my wife and child were recognizably used as extortion. Klaus Bonhoeffer sent out bloody laundry. It is known that Perels was horribly tortured. Walter Bauer, who was in the cell next to mine for a while, asked me to get some poison from Renate's grandfather, Karl Bonhoeffer, who was a medical doctor, because he could not stand it any longer.

Finally now I sent a note for Renate down to the gate asking for a toothbrush. Essentially, Baumer interrogated me about events, meetings, visitors and the content of conversations at the Schleichers' house — but not about any letters from Dietrich Bonhoeffer.

An American Jew recently asked me: "Why didn't you refuse to say anything at all?" That question flabbergasted me. Yes, why didn't I? Of all those in the family who were interrogated, no one simply kept silent. Perhaps my questioner had a simplistic notion of our heroic stand before the commissars. Perhaps he could not sufficiently think his way into the conspiratorial circumstances, under which Bonhoeffer and Dohnanyi had been making statements since April 1943 to cover the continuing conspiracy and deliberately divert attention away from it. As late as fall 1944 we still had some doubts whether the Gestapo knew everything. In fact, each of us still discovered things they did *not* know. So in spite of the situation being much worse, we were all still focused on dissembling and minimizing things. As in the cases of Klaus and Rüdiger, when nothing more could protect them from the worst, a death sentence, they confessed their real motives: "Yes, we conspired, for the sake of the Jews — not only for that reason, but primarily for their sake!" But before death sentences were pronounced, open confession or brave silence would only have harmed other conspirators. In that situation, in which everyone was always trying to protect others, they could not remain silent; they had to cover with talking and lying.

I can hardly place myself in the ranks of those who suffered the most. They paid with death, after having suffered depths of humiliation and being driven to the point of collapse. I was no hero before Baumer and Günther. I followed the family's general line of minimizing as much as possible. In that aforementioned suggestion from Dietrich, he showed me once more what to say. My deferment from regular military service for the *Abwehr* and its activities proved unimportant. I admitted that as a pastor of the Confessing Church I would grant a Jew's request for baptism — Baumer really did ask that question. I described my Lutheran background, according to which a pastor did not interfere in someone else's official duties. Baumer also knew that a Lutheran was supposed to respect what Romans 13 said about being "subject to the governing authorities". He seemed even to have heard something about the "Doctrine of Two Realms" and tried to tie me in with it. I explained how I had tried to be a good soldier, and had even been suggested for officer's training, which he could confirm with my unit in Mantua. And even the commissar found it convincing that my fiancée should be my main interest in going to Schleichers' house. I could not deny that I had met one or another suspect there, as a few notes show which I wrote down after the interrogation: my father-in-law and Klaus Bonhoeffer, earlier also Dietrich and Perels. They talked about the desolate situation after Stalingrad and said that some generals should try to save what could be saved. The commissar tried to get me to admit to conspiratorial ideas emerging from those discussions, but (according to my notes) I said that such ideas only occurred to me "now that we know with hindsight what they were planning". I was a pastor who was only interested in church affairs.

A dangerous moment occurred during my second interrogation. Suddenly Baumer laid a thick transcript on the table and showed me the signature at the back, saying: "Do you know this signature?" It was Dietrich's. Was it going to begin now? So far there had been no mention of the fact that for years I had had a second bed in his room at Marienburger Allee 43. But I knew already that one had to sign seven copies of transcripts. The thought flashed through my mind of how they could distort this material for use in someone else's next interrogation. I can no longer reconstruct the next few minutes. But I must have succeeded in making a convincing impression of my complete ignorance. Baumer soon changed the subject, put the pages away and returned to the Jews and suspicious conversations in No. 42.

But now it was clear. Our secret correspondence to and from Tegel prison was undiscovered and unknown to this group of interrogators, as well as the others at the RSHA. And they never found it.

Even at the RSHA, interdepartmental dynamics caused weak points in the investigation, especially with the growing volume of material on the 20th of July case. In retrospect I know how advantageous the division of labour among the commissars turned out to be for me. Günther and Baumer were responsible for the complex around Rüdiger Schleicher and Klaus Bonhoeffer, and Huppenkothen and Sonderegger were assigned to that around Hans von Dohnanyi and Dietrich Bonhoeffer. Since I was a peripheral figure in the investigation, it never occurred to Baumer to pursue my tiny role in the cases of Dohnanyi and Dietrich Bonhoeffer and what I knew about them. And so he put the transcript away again. Thus my long and close contacts with

Dohnanyi, Perels and even with Dietrich were never investigated. There were no questions about my deferment by the *Abwehr* to the Gossner Mission, my trip to Switzerland in 1942, meetings at the "Fürstenhof" sometimes with Goerdeler, at Ernst von Harnack's, at Marienburger Allee 43.

What they were interested in was the Confessing Church, my feelings of duty towards Jews, my contacts with conspiratorial visitors at No. 42 and my failure to report such friends and relatives.

In the spring of 1945 we were given the name of a People's Court employee, a Dr Heugel, through whom Renate had to apply in Potsdam for a visitor's permit. My formal discharge from the army followed and I was indicted, although I no longer have any paper stating the accusation. Finally I was told that my trial before the Nazi People's Court would take place on May 15, 1945.

But one week before that Germany surrendered, and there was no People's Court any more. Hitler was dead. By then I was riding around on my bicycle between Sakrow and Berlin in a depressing search to discover where and how Rüdiger, Klaus, Perels and Hans John had been killed, on whom the worst Nazi judge, Freisler, had pronounced his last death sentence on February 2. But all that is another story: their deaths, the Lehrterstrasse prison, the unusual inmates there, the bribable, increasingly insecure guards, our fears for survival or non-survival, finally the prison doors opening for the last forty-five of us on April 25, 1945.

Some months later I used the first opportunities to travel west from Berlin with Bishop Dibelius to investigate Dietrich's final fate step by step. Gradually we brought back his letters from Kade and dug up those buried in the garden at Marienburger Allee 42. We put them together with those to his parents, which had passed through the censor and thus did not have to be hidden. Maria von Wedemeyer, Dietrich's fiancée, decided to keep her letters to herself. Some of our smuggled letters in their gas mask containers had become damp and deteriorated. But they had all been transcribed.

Seven years later we held in our hands a selection of his letters from prison, in the form of the book *Widerstand und Ergebung*.[19] And we began to be amazed at the response they evoked around the world.

NOTES

[1] In 1075 Emperor Henry IV (1050-1106) broke with Pope Gregory VII over the issue of "investiture", the right of mediaeval rulers to appoint and install their own bishops. He was excommunicated and declared deposed by Gregory in 1076 but restored after his penance at Canossa. He was excommunicated again in 1080. The investiture conflict continued until the Concordat of Worms in 1122.

[2] *Letters and Papers from Prison*, new edition, New York, Macmillan, 1972, p.358. Hereafter cited as *LPPN*.

[3] "See, the snows on Mount Soratte glare against/ the sky, and the branches strain, giving way/ beneath the weight, and the fluent/ waters stand fast, fixed by the bitter freeze..."

[4] In March 1944, 320 Italians were machine-gunned to death by the SS. This "Massacre of the Ardeatine Caves" was in reprisal for an earlier truck bomb attack by the Resistance which killed 32 Germans in Rome. In 1946 Kesselring was tried and convicted by the British for his connection to the event. Cf. Carlo D'Este, *Fatal Decision: Anzio and the Battle for Rome*, New York, HarperCollins, 1991, pp.307,426.

[5] Cf. Bonhoeffer's diary of his trip to Rome, 14 April 1924; *Dietrich Bonhoeffer Werke*, Vol. 9, p.89.

[6] Benedictine monastery in Bavaria where Bonhoeffer lived from November 1940 to February 1941 while on mission for the *Abwehr* and writing his *Ethics*.

[7] Letter of July 8, 1944; *LPPN*, p.347.

[8] Bonhoeffer's parents lived at Marienburger Allee 43 and the Schleichers next door at 42. Dohnanyis lived in the western suburb of Sakrow, where the family often took refuge from bombing in the city.

[9] Eichkamp was Klaus Bonhoeffer's neighbourhood.

[10] *LPPN*, pp.369f.

[11] *LPPN*, p.375.

[12] Probably "Stations on the Way to Freedom".

[13] Since 1933 Hans von Dohnanyi had collected extensive documentation of Nazi crimes, as well as of the conspiracy. During the war these files were hidden in an armoured file cabinet in the *Abwehr's* underground evacuation site at Zossen, south of Berlin.

[14] *LPPN*, p.385.

[15] *LPPN*, p.394.

[16] *LPPN*, p.396.

[17] *LPPN*, pp.380-85.

[18] Eberhard Bethge, *Dietrich Bonhoeffer*, New York, Harper and Row, 1970, p.797. Leibholz was the husband of Bonhoeffer's twin sister Sabine.

[19] "Resistance and Submission" — the title of the German original of *Letters and Papers from Prison*.

Chapter 5

One of the Silent Bystanders?

Dietrich Bonhoeffer on November 9, 1938

The impetus to look again at the details of where and how
Dietrich Bonhoeffer experienced the *Reichspogromnacht* of
November 9, 1938, and what its consequences were for him, came
from the surprising concern and involvement of the German
public with the fiftieth anniversary of that event. It happened
across the length and breadth of the land, in ecclesiastical, civic
and academic circles, particularly through the searching questions
the youngest generation put to their elders: Where were you
during the arson attacks on the sanctuaries of the God of the
Bible, who is also our God? Where were you when the Torah
scrolls, which also contain our Ten Commandments, were being
publicly desecrated? Where were you during what was obviously
the beginning of the physical destruction of the Jews which we set
in motion in the name of the insane presumption of setting the
world free through the Aryans? Where were you during the wild
acts of revenge, which in spite of their messianic self-confidence in
fact meant enslavement under the false gods of the Germans?

On that day, Dietrich Bonhoeffer and we his colleagues were
not like Pastor Julius van Jan, who immediately told the whole
truth from his village pulpit in Württemberg and was threatened
by demonstrators and reprimanded by his church leadership for
it. We were not like Helmut Gollwitzer. Although he used more
circumspect language, no one listening to his sermon from
Niemöller's pulpit in Dahlem was in doubt about what now to

Originally published in *Erstes Gebot und Zeitgeschichte*, Munich, Chr. Kaiser
Verlag, 1991.

think and to fear. We were not like Karl Immer, who said to his congregation in Wuppertal on November 13: "The question is, how deep do the roots of evil go?" It was clear to everyone who was meant.

So is there a stain left on Bonhoeffer? Might he have been one of the "bystanders", those who looked on and looked away? We do not in fact have any public utterance of Bonhoeffer's about November 9, 1938, either on or after that date. But already in April 1933 he had published an article entitled "The church faced with the Jewish question", in which he went so far as to demand that the church take some kind of action against the first persecutions. (Although this was published in two periodicals, no one took any notice of it, and only a few years ago was it published more widely.) In the summer, he had refused to sign the so-called Bethel Confession, which he himself had helped to draft, because in his view all the references to the basic relationship with Israel, and hence with the Jewish people, had been watered down or removed. As the German pastor in London, he had devoted much of his time and energy to the Jewish emigrants. In the preachers' seminary in Finkenwalde he showed us the first steps on the way to a theology of Israel; and in 1935 he told us: "Only someone who speaks out for the Jews has the right to sing Gregorian chant." (We were in fact enthusiastic about discovering such beauties of the liturgy.) And he was disappointed by every synod of the Confessing Church which again remained silent on the Jewish problem.

What can be reported here is far from any kind of spectacular action, public protest or immediate, decisive change of direction. It is even easy to overlook what we have in writing. Only later did I discover two clues in Bonhoeffer's own hand — a couple of pencil marks and a note in the Bible he used for his daily meditation, and a significant sentence about the event which he inserted into a circular letter for his former students — indicating how he felt about November 9, 1938, and the far-reaching consequences that day had in the ups and downs of his decisions in the resistance conspiracy of the following years.

Thus, November 9 was a decisive point in Bonhoeffer's life and thinking. In this connection we do well to remember something Reinhold Schneider once wrote: "It is not the deed, but the guilty thought that is decisive in every area of Christian life, which means also historical life." [1] It seems to me that the desperate cry in Psalm 74, "O God, how long?", which Bonhoeffer certainly prayed during those days and through which he identified himself with those who were isolated, echoed more strongly in him than the daily radio speeches and newspaper headlines which rang in our ears at that time.

How did those days look for Dietrich Bonhoeffer and for us? What was the situation that we found ourselves in?

Schlönwitz

At that time, Bonhoeffer was teaching in two places, in a clandestine seminary in remote Pomerania, made up of "collective curateships" (the candidates reported to the police as curates while in fact living together in an old mansion) in two neighbouring deaneries. For the first half of the week he taught in the district town of Köslin, not far from the Baltic, halfway between Stettin and Danzig. The other place was 60 kilometres to the east, the little village of Groß-Schlönwitz, where I lived and served as his assistant (supervisor of studies). There he taught during the second half of the week, usually spending the weekends with us. There were a few farms and huts and us in our empty parish house. To the south stretched endless woods and lakes.

November 9, 1938, was a Wednesday. There was nothing unusual in Köslin when Dietrich left at midday, nor was there anything noticeable in Groß-Schlönwitz that evening or during the night. Everything remained quiet. There was a troop of storm-troopers (SA) in Köslin, but there were none in Groß-Schlönwitz — let alone any Jews who might have been attacked. So on the night of November 9 to 10 we probably did not hear a word about Hitler's evening speech in Munich, the pagan ceremonies at the Feldherrnhalle or Goebbels' speech encouraging the SA and the rest of the population to take revenge for the Jewish murder of the German diplomat in Paris, Herr von Rath. It could be that we heard the night-time news broadcast from the BBC on our then very modern and carefully preserved battery receiver. Not until Thursday did the picture of what had happened throughout the Reich filter through to us in that utterly quiet place. That led on Thursday evening to one of those code-laden telephone conversations with Dietrich's parents' house in Berlin, and that in turn to his travelling the 300 kilometres to Berlin.

Although he was prevented by an order of the Gestapo from contacting the council of the Confessing Church, he did get more exact information at his parents' house about what had actually happened, the extent of the actions and the consequences that could be expected after this pogrom.

Today, we can get a more or less accurate picture: according to Heydrich's report to Göring on November 11, 20,000 men (no women yet at that time) were taken to concentration camps. Then it was particularly obvious on the streets, as they had to march between SS-men — unlike what was later done for Auschwitz. According to a report to Göring the following February, 92 Jews had already been murdered; 191 synagogues had been set on fire while the police and fire brigade stood by doing nothing; hundreds of Torah scrolls had been desecrated and destroyed. Following that there were orders for the "Aryanization" of Jewish property, houses, factories, shops; 7500 shops were destroyed and Jews charged for damages or made to sell their houses for below their value. About 120,000 Jews left Germany in the months following November 9, 1938. Even today, groups of young people have difficulty when they ask about the property formerly owned by Jews and try to discover its history.

But back to Groß-Schlönwitz. I accompanied Bonhoeffer on his weekend journey to Berlin. He asked me to go on to Göttingen on November 13 and 14 (he had to return to Köslin to teach), to find out if anything had happened to the house of his sister's family, the Leibholzes, during the pogrom there. In September his sister and her family had emigrated, and we had started them on their way, because the marking of all "non-Aryan" passports was threatening. My notebook contains the timetables and the costs of the sudden journey on November 13 and 14. The house in Göttingen showed no signs of damage from a break-in or terrorist activity.

It is clear that in the first days after November 9 we in Groß-Schlönwitz were completely cut off from the events in the Reich, and only gradually could we get a more complete picture of what had happened. Ours was already a kind of hidden, not to say underground existence. Bonhoeffer himself had no pulpit from which he would have had to say something in a sermon on Sunday November 13. He was not in a position to reflect publicly in a sermon or in parish notices on what could be done. Part of this illegal existence was the understanding that the seminary teaching should not be endangered through courageous public action. So we continued to maintain our daily routine of prayer, meditation, seminars and lectures.

Köslin

When Bonhoeffer came back to teach in Köslin on November 14, he found a situation different from that in Groß-Schlönwitz. Since the previous Wednesday night, the theological students of the district town had heard one way or another about the burning of the synagogues, and after the Nazi period one of them wrote about Bonhoeffer's arrival in this situation:

> A great discussion now arose among us about this deed, and how to assess it. Meanwhile Dietrich Bonhoeffer had returned. Some of us spoke of the curse which had haunted the Jews since Jesus' death on the cross. Bonhoeffer rejected this with extreme sharpness... He utterly refused to see in the destruction of the synagogues by the Nazis a fulfilment of the curse on the Jews. This was a case of sheer violence. "If the synagogues burn today, the churches will be on fire tomorrow."[2]

That group of theological students, who had been in Bonhoeffer's class only a few weeks, certainly represented fairly accurately what was then thought or not thought about Jews in the Confessing Church. Bonhoeffer knew full well the uncertainty that attended any attempt to situate this event in a faith and theology full of anti-Judaism. A theology of the punishment of Israel and its replacement had been dominant for centuries. The theory of a curse was also mentioned in this Köslin circle with reference to Matthew 27:25, "His blood be on us and on our children," as Maltusch pointedly emphasizes in his report. Bonhoeffer sharply turned on the suggestion that it was possible here to argue theologically in terms of God's anger. First, the only thing to talk about was human behaviour, that is, the violence of the Nazi regime and the co-responsibility of non-Nazis.

Today it is difficult to imagine how the centuries-old notions of divine curse, punishment and replacement were taken for granted even by us in the Confessing Church. Of course, we set no synagogues afire. We were completely unaware that Martin Luther had once suggested something similar; for Luther's writings on the Jews were not included in the four-volume edition of Clemen, the textbook on Luther's writings used for exams at that time. Julius Streicher was the first to make them known, and in 1937 the Kaiser Verlag remedied the deficiency and published a supplementary volume with Luther's anti-Jewish writings.

No, we did not act like Nazis against the Jews. But what about November 9 with its regimented popular anger, when Hitler turned thousands of Germans across the length and breadth of the land into instruments of God's wrath on the Jews? How was that to be judged? As we will see, Bonhoeffer was already clearly thinking along other lines, moving towards a theology of Israel of a sort that scarcely anyone else at that time was thinking or talking about.

Psalm 74

And that brings us to the pencil marks in Bonhoeffer's Bible and to the sentence he inserted in his circular letter, the two documented signs of a reaction. In the Luther Bible which he used daily, beside Psalm 74:8, there is the date "9.11.38" with an exclamation mark and several lines against the following verses, all in his own hand:

> They said to themselves, "We will utterly subdue them";
> they burned all the meeting places of God in the land.
> We do not see our emblems;
> there is no longer any prophet,
> and there is no one among us who knows how long.
> How long, O God, is the foe to scoff?
> Is the enemy to revile your name forever?
> Why do you hold back your hand;
> why do you keep your hand in your bosom?

Bonhoeffer made these pencil marks and wrote the date at that time. This was not a note added as a result of later reflection. This is clear from the evidence of one of the Groß-Schlönwitz theological students, Hans Werner Jensen from Kiel, who then wrote the date November 10, 1938, as a note next to Psalm 74:8 in his Bible. Thus it was right in the midst of the realization in the Schlönwitz parish house of the first dreadful news that this Bible text was under discussion. And Bonhoeffer had recommended it for meditation. I cannot say how he came on that verse then, but it obviously struck him during the communal praying of the Psalms. (During the morning and evening prayer in the seminary the whole Psalter was used — nothing was left out.) He was struck by the shattering experience of abandonment felt by the desperate victims of the pogrom two-and-a-half millennia earlier, when the Babylonians laid waste the Temple and deported the people; and now, through the strength of his identification with them, he was similarly struck by the acute and real cries of abandonment of that night in 1938. He was struck by the lament "O God, how long?", and probably also added in his mind the note: O God, how long can I stand by and watch?

This notation of "9.11.38" in the margin of the Bible Bonhoeffer used daily is something unique. There are pencil lines marking verses and words on many pages and also occasionally a note regarding a parallel passage and even the odd reference to the verse number of a hymn. But apart from Psalm 74:8, there is not a single note in his Bible giving a date or key word for something contemporary or of political or family or personal importance. This indicates the extent to which he was disturbed and that he had the beginnings of an idea that this could be an ultimate challenge: this day of persecution might determine his vocation and his fate.

It should not be forgotten how Bonhoeffer used his Bible for prayer. He thought that one should sit and listen prayerfully to the Bible, to hear whatever voice would speak. This meant that the I, the Today, the contemporary world and their voices had to remain silent, so that the person praying would become immersed in the world of the biblical verse and thus become involved in biblical salvation history. This is similar to how Jews read the story of the liberation from Egypt and the time in which they read it. And so when he was praying with the Scriptures, Bonhoeffer never actually referred to his world, with its dates and catchwords, in his marginal jottings, although he always had a pencil in his hand to mark things in the printed word that became important — that is, with the exception of this one occasion in Psalm 74:8.

Circular letter

Now to the sentence he included in his circular letter dated November 20, 1938. Circular letters went out to former students every two months. Since the establishment of the "communal curateship" at the end of 1937, these letters were written only by Bonhoeffer; and since Goebbels' prohibition of circular letters on July 30, 1937, they were no longer called the "Finkenwalde Circular Letter", but were registered as personal letters and signed by hand. This particular letter of November 20 had already been planned as an Advent letter and dealt mainly with the idea of patience, which had been the subject for New Testament study in the seminary and was now seen in the context of the weakening of the illegal church as a result of the offer of legalization to church groups loyal to the state. Into this Bonhoeffer inserted one sentence which referred to the events of November 9 and which gives an indication of his reaction, stimulating a complete theology of Israel in contrast to the time, and communicating his own involvement as well. This sentence, whose depth and implications perhaps only really came through to us much later, runs as follows: "During the last few days I have been thinking a lot about Psalm 74, Zechariah 2:8, Romans 9:3f. and 11:11-15. That really makes one pray."[3]

Here every word carries weight, from "during the last few days" to "really makes one pray." Bonhoeffer shared guidelines from the Scriptures with his brothers and friends in order to help them to cope with events, reinterpreting statements of faith in the light of the new situation, and in a way that no one else in Germany was doing at that time. In Holland there was already the voice of K.H. Miskotte, in Switzerland that of Karl Barth, but who could — or wanted to — read such things then in the Reich? And then the emotionally laden sharing of insights about his prayer: it was not until later in retrospect that we really recognized its full meaning, which was only possible after the later stages of his journey became known.

A close examination of the Bible references in these three lines leads to some surprising observations. They do not appear in Bonhoeffer's earlier work, at least not in the way they are read and used here. Even less did they have a place in the awareness of the church, not even the Confessing Church. Psalm 74 had never been referred to until then. He mentions it now to the Finkenwalde students not so that they can study the Hebrew text but to invite them to pray it along with him if they dare — the need for "daring" would not be because of the Gestapo, but because of the anti-Jewish theological assumptions already solidified within them.

Bonhoeffer had in fact used the text from Zechariah 2:8 — "the one who touches you touches the apple of my eye" — in his December 1937 circular letter. He had at that time taken the texts for the day at the end of the year as the basis of short reflections; and the text for December 28, 1937, had been this passage. But then he had applied the comforting message exclusively to the persecuted church. It must be remembered that the list of petitionary prayers of the *Bruderrat* at the end of 1937 had become longer than ever before or since; moreover, 27 of the brothers of the Finkenwalde community had been imprisoned during Advent.[4] One of them was Bonhoeffer's close colleague Fritz Onnasch, whom he had just visited in his cell in Stettin, and the visit had affected him deeply. So this single previous meditation on Zechariah made no reference to the Jews in Nazi Germany. Now, scarcely a year later, it is very different: Bonhoeffer reads the text and teaches it to those to whom he is writing unambiguously and exclusively in terms of its validity for the Jews, leaving no room for a theology of punishment and excluding the idea that punishment, if that were a reality, could be brought about through the "Aryans".

He reads Romans 9:3f. in a similar way: "They are Israelites, and to them belong the adoption, the glory, the covenants, the giving of the law, the worship and the promises." This passage is found here and there in his earlier writings. One example is found in the context of statements about the Bethel Confession[5] in 1933, when Bonhoeffer was working on the draft and then, of course, withdrew his signature when the statements about the Jews were completely watered down or left out of the final version.[6] Another example is his teaching after the Steglitz Confessing Synod of 1936-37. But now, in 1938, he reads and teaches about this text in order flatly to contradict the church's centuries-old teaching of the rejection of the Jews, being so moved that he asks how church teaching could so long have completely forgotten this statement from Paul about the continuing existence of Judaism.

And it is similar with the fourth text, Romans 11:11-15. In this, Paul bears witness to Israel's final acceptance as "life from the dead" and connects its acceptance with the final reconciliation of the world, so that it too might belong to the God of the first commandment.

This consideration of the use of the four texts significantly mentioned in his letter demonstrates the importance to Bonhoeffer of the events of November 1938 and shows that his apparently harmless use of these quotations is in fact a very important new stage in his interpretation. No longer does he just read statements about the Israel of the past as referring to the church; rather, he now hears statements about the Jews who are at present being reviled, about the continuing people of God.

Today we know what an immense step forward that was. Then when we read Bonhoeffer's circular letter of November 20, we scarcely understood this new way of reading. But Bonhoeffer wrote that he had "reflected a great deal about it". And only decades later did we discover that he had already written in his *Ethikfragment* of 1940: "A rejection of the Jews from the West must bring after it a rejection of Christ, for Christ was a Jew."[7]

Bonhoeffer intended these biblical verses of November 20, 1938, to be aids to understanding for his students, but not only as a stimulus to discussion. With noticeable commitment he adds: "That really makes one pray." Why "really"? I can hear an undertone of a certain despair here, and also the inkling of the approaching inevitable decisions. What sort of prayer had it brought him to? I think one can know to a certain extent what was at the centre of his prayer.

Two things in particular must have concerned him. First of all, the role of the ordained preacher of unbounded salvation in a church which existed and exercised its office so far from the hunted Jews. Can this role be fulfilled without solidarity with them? Can one continue in this calling without some changes?

Second, it seems to me that Bonhoeffer's attention was caught by the double "how long?" of Psalm 74. When will there be an end to the pogrom? How will an end come about? What role will fall to me in it? What will be the cost to Christians of having allowed things to come to the point of November 9?

Today we know what his answer to the question of the Psalm turned out to be: beginning in 1940 to collaborate in the conspiracy. Of course, there were many different and shaky steps in between.

The stages

Even in the days immediately surrounding November 9, 1938, Bonhoeffer knew through his brother-in-law Hans von Dohnanyi, to whom he was close and who was then in the Ministry of Justice, about early plans for a coup after the annexation of Austria and during the Sudeten crisis. In Bonhoeffer's family, there was at times even too much optimism about a coup, which was connected with his answer to the Psalm's "how long?". Could new plans one day mean Dietrich Bonhoeffer's own personal participation?

But were there not perhaps still possibilities of corporate action within the church? Was another corporate act possible like the astonishing Confessing Synod of Barmen in 1934, highly political in spite of its non-political intentions? But the Confessing Church had reached a low point in its progressive weakening, perhaps in its blindness too.

In 1938, three fatal defeats had silenced the Confessing Church. After the annexation of Austria, the official state church ordered the pastors to take an oath of allegiance to Hitler as a birthday present for the *Führer*. When, after initial resistance, almost all the pastors of the Confessing Church in normal parishes had also sworn the oath, a communiqué came in August from party headquarters saying that Hitler had never wanted this oath from them and placed no value on it. Then, in late summer, the so-called intact church dissociated itself from the *Bruderrat* of the destroyed church when it published a liturgy with penitential prayers for the preservation of peace, and the weekly SS-paper *Schwarzes Korps* attacked them as betrayers of the fatherland in the battle of Sudetenland. And finally, the church of the *Bruderrat* publicly dissociated itself from Karl Barth, when he wrote to his colleague, Professor Josef Hromádka in Prague, that Hitler's attack should be resisted and that such a call to arms should be made in the name of the church of Jesus Christ.

No, these weeks did not invite trust in the corporate authority of a clear statement of a Confessing Synod or its organs. There was no answer in sight to the question "how long?", except through completely different commitments, different people, different authority figures, different means. Could responsibility in the matter of the pogrom still be placed on many shoulders? Individual assumption of responsibility without previous justification and assurances was coming nearer and nearer. It is this situation which is reflected in Bonhoeffer's pencilled notations next to Psalm 74 during the week of the pogrom. It implies that the road ahead could be long and new and by no means straightforward. What began in thinking and prayer ended in action and death. The days in remote Pomerania in November 1938 were its first stage, and it found expression in the short sigh: "That really makes one pray."

Another stage on the way to an answer to the "how long?" came with Bonhoeffer's journey to the USA in summer 1939. We can sympathize with the fact that he was still exploring the possibilities of finding a completely different role in the USA far away from the land of November 9. When he discovered after a few weeks there that every possibility of work was open to him, but that in accepting it he would be taking away a post from a poor Jewish immigrant without a work permit, he turned back in the direction of his own self-destructive homeland: "Since I've been on the ship, my inner tension about the future has stopped."[8]

When he became actively involved in the work of the conspiracy in 1940, about two years after November 9, he formulated a confession of guilt, the product of a maturing process which had begun with praying Psalm 74 and the note in his circular letter of 1938. Here is explicit mention of a double subject: "I confess" and "the church confesses". The confession contained, among other things:

> The church confesses to having seen the irrational use of brutal violence, the physical and spiritual suffering of innumerable innocent people, oppression, hate and murder, without having raised its voice on their behalf, without having found a way to hasten to their aid. It has become responsible for destroying the lives of the weakest and most defenseless brothers of Jesus Christ.[9]

Bonhoeffer wrote that in autumn 1940 before Auschwitz had even started. November 9, 1938, had already been more than enough. He wrote it before the beginning of the systematic deportation to the east in autumn 1941, when he became involved in activities to save individuals, as in the case of "U7",[10] when the resistance saved a few Jews by smuggling them into Switzerland. The concreteness of this 1940 confession of guilt was not even attained by the German church when it voiced its Stuttgart confession of guilt in October 1945.

A public answer to the torturous question "how long?" came on July 20, 1944, with the coup — and that failed. But nevertheless Bonhoeffer saw it as an answer in which he knew that he had been a part. On July 21, in his cell in Tegel, he wrote a poem about the liberating answer which rang out loud and clear even in failure. It was a poem about the price which that answer exacted, but even more about the way in which that answer ended in one stroke the twilight and torture of the long road to an answer. The last verse of the poem, "Stages on the Way to Freedom", has the heading "Death" and reads as follows:

> Come now, highest of feasts on the way to freedom eternal,
> Death, strike off the fetters, break down the walls
> Of our mortal body and our blinded soul,
> That we may see at last the sight which here we could not see.
> Freedom, we sought you long, in discipline, action, suffering.
> Now, as we die, we see and know you at last, face to face.[11]

The "freedom eternal" includes earthly liberation, as Bonhoeffer implies in a letter a week later, that is to say, liberation from the crushing contamination of having been a bystander, an onlooker, of having looked away.

For Bonhoeffer, it was not just any death or every death, but this particular death, which was intended to be a public and shameful death, that meant the irrevocable liberation from personal and corporate complicity in the murders of November 9, 1938, and from Auschwitz. This death ended once and for all, publicly, the consistent betrayal of the victims of November 9 and of Auschwitz.

For Hitler, this death was an act of vengeance. He ordered it still April 5, 1945. For Bonhoeffer, it was God's judgment on the all-too-long interval between November 9, 1938, and July 20, 1944. And yet his death already overtook the signs of Hitler's power. It was a death which fulfilled "our desire that it should not catch up with us by chance, or suddenly, or without any significance, but in the fullness of life and in complete commitment... It will not be external circumstances but we ourselves who make of our death what it can be, a death freely and willingly accepted."[12]

To summarize: November 9, 1938, in the remote Pomeranian village and Psalm 74; the astonishing return in 1939 from the USA; the confession of guilt after Hitler's greatest victories in France and at the time of his first involvement in the conspiracy; the poem of July 21, 1944, and its context – all this looks to us now like an exciting continuity. For Bonhoeffer himself, however, it was hardly ever clear and decisive. But his identification with the desperate and the God-forsaken in 1938, through his prayerful involvement with the victims of the pogroms of 2500 years earlier, remained the decisive impetus of his life.

NOTES

1 *Verhüllter Tag*, Hegner, 1954, p.212.
2 Gottfried Maltusch, in W.D. Zimmermann, *I Knew Dietrich Bonhoeffer*, London: Collins, and New York, Harper and Row, 1966, 1973, p.150.
3 *Gesammelte Schriften*, II, p.544.
4 Cf. *Biography*, p.659.
5 The Bethel Confession was drawn up in August 1933 by a small group, including Bonhoeffer, acting on behalf of the opposition group within the newly established *Reichskirche*. Its purpose was to provide support to groups attempting to resist the pro-Nazi trend in the church. However, when the initial draft was watered down to draw wider support, Bonhoeffer refused to sign it. In its initial form it could be considered a forerunner to the Barmen Declaration one year later.
6 Cf. Christine-Ruth Müller, *Bekenntnis und Bekennen: Dietrich Bonhoeffer in Bethel 1933*, Munich, 1989, pp.70f.
7 *Ethik*, Neuausgabe, p.95.
8 *Gesammelte Schriften*, I, p.315.
9 *Ethik*, p.121f.
10 "U7" or "Unternehmen 7" ("Enterprise 7") was the code name for a secret rescue operation smuggling 12-15 Jews into Switzerland. The operation was carried out by the *Abwehr* (the German Intelligence Service), particularly by its chief, Admiral Canaris, and Hans von Dohnanyi, both members of the resistance.
11 *Widerstand und Ergebung*, p.403.
12 "After Ten Years", WEN, p.26.

Chapter 6

Marienburger Allee 43

The House, Its Family and Guests

My claim to speak here about "the house, its family and guests" is somewhat weak in the presence of the very competent grandchildren of Paula and Karl Bonhoeffer: Christine Korenke-Schleicher, Dorothee Bracher-Schleicher, Marianne Leibholz, Barbara Bayer-Dohnanyi and Renate Bethge-Schleicher. They know more! Especially about the continuity between the Wangenheimstrasse, the family home from 1916-1935, and the Marienburger Allee. They know the details, the daily goings-on then taken for granted which today, four or five decades later, have to be described. They will quickly register distortions, exaggerations and omissions, and they have a sure sense of what is important and what is secondary. They remember the parties and the funny moments. And today their emotions run deeper than mine. I advise you to use the occasion to make them talk and to put questions to them. You will witness a quick-tongued competition about who remembers this and who forgot that. Marianne, for instance, could still recite entire parts of the poems that she and her cousins offered for the 60th birthday of their grandmother Paula Bonhoeffer on December 30, 1936.

The time which legitimizes my claim to speak began only at Christmas 1935, when Dietrich, returning to the newly established home for the first time from the illegal Confessing Church seminary in Finkenwalde, brought with him this country boy

---

Address at the inauguration on June 1, 1987, of the meeting- and memorial-centre in the house where Karl and Paula Bonhoeffer lived and their son Dietrich maintained a room in the attic, where he lived and worked until his arrest in April 1943.

from the Saxony province. Later I found myself here with him for days or weeks, upstairs in his attic room (we were both late sleepers!). That was, for instance, during the uncertain weeks at the end of 1937 when the Gestapo had sealed our seminary and we had to invent the *Sammelvikariate*.[1] Justus Perels often joined us when we discussed the next steps.[2] Another time was in the spring and summer of 1940, after the final dissolution of the seminary, when Dietrich and I were trying to figure out what to do next, delaying a decision in the vain hope for a *putsch*, thinking that Hitler might be defeated in France. You should also realize that the window of that room looked out over the garden of the neighbouring house at number 42, where the presence of the Schleicher children became for me more and more exciting and attractive, and which eventually led to my partial claim to speak here today!

Conscious of such limitations and in the presence of undisputed authorities, let me nevertheless make three remarks about the theme "the house, its family and guests": the first concerning the relation between the Prinz-Albrecht-Strasse and the Marienburger Allee; then remembering the people who lived in or frequented this house; and finally something about the spirit of this house, transmitted to our benefit and embodied by one or the other of the members of the family.

Two memorials

It is significant that two things are presently happening in Berlin, fatefully inter-related despite their asymmetry, and thus very important for an adequate reception of the heritage represented here. One is the preservation of the meagre remains of the *Reichssicherheitshauptamt*[3] at the Prinz-Albrecht-Strasse, the place J. Tuchel has called the "headquarters of terror"; the other is the renovation and preservation of private homes such as this one, homes which are memorable not so much for their architecture but rather for the families which lived there, in our case for the spirit of a particularly great family and its contribution to the history of our country and its church.

The preservation of each serves to perpetuate the spirit that reigned within its walls, preventing any dilution of the radically different ways in which their respective inhabitants lived and worked in them. As physically fixed points they resist any self-serving modification of their lines.

For that was how things were: *there* was the centre to assure
the security of the Third Reich — corridors and halls, whole
floors of generals and planners, equipped with files and torture
chambers, staffing the various command and executive organs.
Every conceivable means for the official exercise of power was at
their disposal, from access to the precious gasoline and the right
of way in traffic and telecommunications, to the necessary
recruiting and training authority for the surveillance of the
people and the system, all the way to the right to enter any
private home. All their time was devoted to this; they had
nothing else to do.

And *here* was one of the weak centres for the destabilization of
the Third Reich — a family residence, established in 1935 as the
home of a retired professor of medicine, a gathering place for the
families of each of the seven children. The sons and sons-in-law
had very different professional involvements — Karl-Friedrich, a
physicist in Leipzig; Klaus, a lawyer at Lufthansa; Ursula's
husband at the ministry of aviation; Christel's husband at the
justice ministry; Sabine with her husband banned from the university; Susanne's husband at the forbidden *Kirchliche Hochschule*
(church seminary); Dietrich as director of an illegal pastoral
training school — but all were fundamentally united in the effort
to contribute to the undesired and unrehearsed resistance against
everything the *Reichssicherheitshauptamt* stood for. Theirs were
part-time activities in the underground, so to say, without any
official support. In 1946 Christel wrote about the unequal
struggle:

> I believe that during the last years the SS won out over the resisters
> not least because of their superior technical means. They had every-
> thing that these people would have needed and whose procurement
> caused them endless difficulties, involving detours and the breaking
> of rules. Moreover, each attempt increased the mistrust and the
> vigilance of the other side. Think only of the difficulty of procuring
> explosives.

Marienburger Allee 43 was certainly in no way a headquarters,
but it was a centre, continually devoted to a culture from which it
never allowed itself to be alienated and which it was bent on
preserving under all circumstances for the benefit of others. A
refuge and resource for energy to hold out and to motivate ever

anew. A centre as Dietrich described it in his famous baptism letter from Tegel, or about which he wrote compellingly in the essay "After Ten Years", which he drafted here in 1942.

Prinz-Albrecht-Strasse 8 and Marienburger Allee 43: now they are monuments in the literal sense, testimonies to the unequal struggle. They illustrate the different bases from which each side engaged in the deadly conflict. They prove to be indispensable manifestations of one of the most ominous chapters of our history. Who stood against whom? What should live again and what not?

Those who visited the house

Whom do we remember of the people who frequented this house and who contributed to its profile? We have to realize that at the moment the family took up residence here, the second climax of the persecution of the Jews, the proclamation of the Nuremberg laws, had already been reached. Each of the seven sisters and brothers had friends among those who fell under the legislation concerning "non-Aryans" and shared in the pain of their expulsion and emigration. Only Franz Hildebrandt, the incomparable friend of Dietrich and ever-patient uncle of the grandchildren, went in and out of the house for a year-and-a-half, until he too left the country in 1937.[4] Starting in 1933, all the sisters and brothers had to resist the "Aryanization" of juridical theory and practice, of medicine and physics and, most spectacularly, of gospel and church.

It had been foreseen from the start that the Schleichers would be the neighbours in number 42. Among other things they took charge of the musical life of the family, organizing, for instance, a performance of Haydn's Symphony for Children or the Walcha Cantata for Karl Bonhoeffer's 75th birthday, just a few days before the arrests on April 5, 1943. It was in number 42, where Dietrich was visiting his sister Ursula, that Röder and Sonderegger found him, and where for the last time he enjoyed his sister's excellent cooking until his father had to hand him over to the bailiffs. It was also at his sister's that the Gestapo arrested Klaus on October 1, 1944; with his sister and her husband, who was fetched three days later, he struggled with the decision of whether to go underground, commit suicide or surrender. It was also in that house that a few weeks later I discussed testimonies for the impending trials before I followed Klaus and Rüdiger into the prison on Lehrterstrasse 3.

The plans for number 43 included an apartment for the grandmother, the remarkable 90-year old Julie Bonhoeffer-Tafel, as well as an attic room for Dietrich whenever he returned home, especially after he was forbidden in 1937 to stay in Berlin "on business". Following the grandmother's death in January 1936, the Leibholz family used the apartment when visiting from England where they had emigrated. At the outbreak of the war the five members of the Dohnanyi family squeezed into those rooms until they could move to Sakrow on the Havel.

All of them brought along old acquaintances as well as new friends: Hans Oster, Josef Mueller, Bernd Gisevius and Schmidhuber; but also Nikolaus von Halem, Freiherr von Guttenberg, Ernst von Harnack (of course both: the conservative and the socialist); Pater Johannes from Ettal; Klaus's friends, the brothers John and Josef Wirmer and Kurt Wergin; Hans Schoenfeld and Paula Bonhoeffer's cousin, General von Hase. From ecumenical Geneva came Professor Courvoisier, Nils Ehrenström and Birger Forell; among the proven colleagues of father Bonhoeffer was Ferdinand Sauerbruch. One day, on April 7, 1940, Friederich von Bodelschwingh and Paul Braune-Lobethal discussed with Karl Bonhoeffer what could be done for the epileptic inmates of their institutions who were threatened by government-imposed measures of euthanasia.

When Dietrich was placed under an extradition order, he took the precaution of seeing his friends from the *Bruderrat* in this house: Wilhelm Jannasch, Hans Lockies, Willy Rott and especially Oskar Hammelsbeck, who reported later that already before 1943 he had discussed with Dietrich in the attic room questions about a responsible relation between church and world.[5] There were frequent visits from Friedrich Justus Perels, first to discuss the issues raised by the Synod of Dahlem, later to plan the rescue of Jewish citizens, finally to discuss problems related to the covering up of the *putsch* and those arising from the arrests, especially in his role as mediator between the family and the military judge Karl Sack. And let us not forget the Finkenwalde students, among whom word had gotten around that good advice and support was to be had not only from

Dietrich but even more from his mother. Here in this house the bailiffs confiscated on that April day in 1943 the manuscripts of the *Ethics* — which they returned, however, the explosive nature of their contents having remained hidden from them.

In the basement of number 42 the parents survived the Soviet attacks, together with Emmi Bonhoeffer, her brother Justus Delbrück, the Steltzers, the Carl Diem family and myself. Missing were Klaus and Rüdiger, of whose assassination we soon learned, and Hans Dohnanyi and Dietrich. Maria von Wedemeyer, Dietrich's fiancée, who for months had been a support to the parents, was at that time in southern Germany in a vain search for traces of Dietrich.

Two men who came to this house soon after the end of the war must be mentioned. One was George Bell, Bishop of Chichester. Dietrich's parents were the first people he saw during his first visit to Berlin in October 1945, and he received from them the copy of the *Imitatio Christi* which Dietrich had kept with him in his cell. The other was Reinhold Niebuhr, who met the couple, battered but unbent, and, if I remember correctly, conversed with them in German during tea on the veranda near the garden.

Finally, we remember the moving reunion of all the surviving members of the family in a scantily repaired house, especially the visit of the emigrated Leibholz sister and brother, for the last festive occasions in March 1948: the golden anniversary of the parents and Karl Bonhoeffer's 80th birthday.

A unique atmosphere

I would like to recall the unique atmosphere created by the inhabitants who filled the house by citing three texts. They speak about Dietrich, Christel and Gerhard Leibholz, but they also apply in one way or another to their siblings and parents, since their reactions to events resemble each other.

Erich Fromm wrote to Hans Jürgen Schultz in 1973:

After having read almost all of Bonhoeffer's letters, I would like to thank you once more, not only for having bought me the book but also for having provided the opportunity for an exceptional experience. The wisdom, depth and strength of this man are unique and deeply moving.

And after raising a few questions about a perhaps authoritarian image of God, the role of women and of the elites, Fromm continues:

> It seems to me that this [Bonhoeffer's stature] really represents the flowering of German culture, shaped over centuries and finding its expression in such persons. Will there be a continuation of this German tradition? Or is it dead like most of the noble things in our contemporary world?

The second quotation comes from the funeral oration for Dietrich's sister Christine von Dohnanyi in February 1965.[6] Those in the know will recognize the traits described here also in the other women of the family, especially in the mistress of the house, Paula Bonhoeffer. The insight and formulation stem from Renate Bethge, for whom Christine von Dohnanyi was her favourite aunt:

> She was marvellous in her house. Although untiring, she was never rushed. It never seemed that there was much to be done. When she entered the room, dullness disappeared.
>
> She was wonderful in freely expressing her just and unerring anger. She permitted herself to be honestly angry. Her critique was precise and straightforward. She kept away from the infamy and the shabbiness of her days.
>
> She preserved the sovereignty of someone who is well informed. She never lost her intense interest in public affairs, nor the capacity to anticipate all the possible and impossible constellations. While she could not change the fate of being at the mercy of others, she was privileged by the freedom of spirit.
>
> Once she wrote of her father that "he was a rock when he was needed". This also applies to herself. I am thinking of the critical moments of the *Kirchenkampf*. All of us are aware of what she did for Germany — although she would never acknowledge it. We all sought her quick and yet well-founded advice which always pointed to a way out! And what an image she left us of reserve and dignity when she was faced with inhumanity. When and of whom has the utmost ever been demanded as it was of her and her family — over tormenting months and years and under ambiguous circumstances? Occasionally she could elaborately discuss secondary matters, but the really important things received only rare mention, if at all. Perhaps we did not always and in everything understand her; but we admired and loved her.

The third text concerns Gerhard Leibholz:

Looking for the ground of such radiance and charm on the part of this cultivated scholar, academic teacher and impeccable judge, we find first of all that his whole being was determined by a nowadays rare noblesse. Whatever he said was credible, because everyone who met him felt that his words corresponded to an inner conviction and were borne out by his actions. A sovereign manner, accompanied by modesty, lent him an inevitable and natural authority and distance. While being decisive on the issues, he emanated for all who knew him amiable tolerance and generosity as well as unassuming warmth and calm — even in the stress of affairs, a testimony to the spirit of a man who knew that in the last analysis the world is integrated in and held up by a metaphysical order that transcends the here and now. This is how he will be remembered by all who have met and known him.[7]

This was the spirit of all who lived in this house; it was the spirit of this house. It will survive the demons of that other centre which boasted everlasting power! To go and visit that centre will always be a *duty*; but to visit this house will always be a joy.

NOTES

[1] These were "illegal" groups of seven to ten candidates for the ministry, living in a pastor's manse and working in the surrounding area while being taught by Bonhoeffer. They ended in 1940 when Bonhoeffer decided to join the resistance movement.

[2] Perels was juridical counsellor of the Confessing Church in Berlin and a member of the resistance movement. Arrested in 1944, he was tortured and murdered in April 1945.

[3] Central office of the Gestapo and the SS.

[4] Hildebrandt, a New Testament scholar of Jewish origin, was a colleague of Bonhoeffer in Finkenwalde and of Martin Niemöller. In 1937 he went to London, where he worked in the German-speaking parish. Together with Bishop G. Bell he conducted the memorial service for Bonhoeffer in July 1945 at Holy Trinity Church in London.

[5] Cf. O. Hammelsbeck, "Mit Bonhoeffer im Gespräch", in *Begegnungen*, pp.169-80.

[6] Christine von Dohnanyi wrote an important aide-mémoire on the activities of her husband Hans, who was, together with Oster, the most important collaborator with Colonel-General Beck in preparing the assassination attempt on Hitler on July 20, 1944. Hans von Dohnanyi was hanged in 1945.

[7] H.-J. Rink, "Richterbilder: In memoriam Gerhard Leibholz", *Jahrbuch des Öffentlichen Rechts der Gegenwart*, new series, Vol. 35, Tübingen, 1986, p.142.

Chapter 7

Bonhoeffer's Theology
of Friendship

This is a late moment for me to deal with this topic. Having
never taken it up in decades of working on, with and for Dietrich
Bonhoeffer, I have now, in my eighties, been asked twice recently
to talk biographically about the stages of our friendship. The first
time was in the joyful circumstances of an after-dinner speech at
Union Theological Seminary in New York. Now I will talk about
this in the circumstances of an academic series from Aristotle to
Moltmann, with its daunting level of expectation and under
pressure of time to cover a far too multi-faceted topic. But I do so
with a certain pleasure in the personal charms of the topic.

Why so late? There are two simple reasons. The first: How
could one of the participants discuss the subject dispassionately
and appropriately? The second: There used to be understandable
jealousy among Bonhoeffer's surviving former seminary students
from Finkenwalde. I wonder if there still is. This could possibly
have damaged our efforts centrally to collect and evaluate the
Bonhoeffer sources, for a discussion of the topic of friendship
could not avoid the difference between friendship in the general
sense of having "friends" in all sorts of different historical,
professional and geographical locations, and friendship in the
sense of relationships with each individual "best friend". In this
latter sense there were four "singular" friends.

Dietrich Bonhoeffer also took up this topic explicitly and
intentionally only very late in his life. He was interested in

Lecture given on April 7, 1993, at the Institute for Philosophy and Religion,
Boston University, Boston, Massachusetts, USA, in a series on concepts of
friendship.

communio from the very beginning, but always as an ecclesiological issue. At the same time, it is impossible to imagine him without his friends. For someone of his temperament, they were essential to his very life. But there is not a single passage in any of his own books in which he wrote a specific analysis of the place and dignity of friendship, whether sociologically, psychologically, philosophically or theologically.

Although the sources we have on this subject come only from his time in prison from 1943 on, they do seem to me to have a concentrated power. They speak primarily of friendship in the singular, not as a form of socialization among many other structures of life. He probably felt some urgency to bring intellectually formulated clarity to that which he had personally experienced and possessed so generously. Did he want, on the one hand, to learn to deal better with a situation which had become precarious and dangerous for him and his partner in the 1940s? For seven months in 1943, during his interrogations in prison, he had avoided any mention of me, and no correspondence between us was possible. Was there a life-giving strength in the friendship, needed now more than ever, good fortune in the midst of misfortune, which he was trying to think through? On the other hand, just at that time a problem had arisen which called for objective treatment: I had just been married and he was preparing to be married, having become engaged in January 1943; and our friendship would certainly have undergone a mutation.

What we find from the time of his imprisonment are four qualitatively different salient sources:

1. *Fiction fragments.* In the summer and fall of 1943 Dietrich tried his hand at writing a drama and a novel. Pairs of friends play a role in both fragments. It is clear that concrete autobiographical experiences influenced both the portrayal of the friendships and the reflection on them found in these fragments. In the novel, in addition, there is a singular-type school friendship, which proceeds from a perilously competitive relationship through a tempestuous crisis to a deep, responsible alliance. No evidence of a situation comparable to this theme of conflict is found in Bonhoeffer's own biographical experiences of singular friendship.

2. *The letter.* The second and most important source is a portion of Bonhoeffer's letter to me from prison on January 23, 1944.[1] It attempts to make up for something he had not thought

about at all a few years earlier when he was working on his *Ethics*. Now he was seeking a possible theological and sociological integration of friendship into the four divine mandates of Christian life (church, state, work, family) — or possibly not — by adding that "broad area of freedom", which the church was providing in 1943.

3. *Stifter*. The third source is a small anthology of the writings of the nineteenth-century Austrian author Adalbert Stifter, which was sent into Tegel prison for Bonhoeffer to read and then returned to his parents' home. It delivered news for me in the form of a message in secret code, and contained his pencil markings in the margins of passages by Stifter on the uniqueness of the phenomenon of friendship.

4. *The poem*. Finally, Dietrich sent me an intensely reflective poem, "The Friend", for my birthday in August 1944. It was an unequalled birthday present for me, just at the point that our communication would reach its permanent end.

In fact, there was a fifth source, written during the same winter of 1943-1944. Bonhoeffer called it a "small literary piece", inspired by our recent coming together in November and December 1943, on the "meeting between two old friends after a long separation during the war".[2] It cost him, as he wrote, "more time than I thought at first". At the end of February he thought he would soon have it finished. In early July he admitted that "the small piece" was "not yet quite finished". Unfortunately, nothing from this fragment ever reached us. But his interim reports on it show at least how much the topic occupied Bonhoeffer, both thematically and personally, since our reunion. Evidently, he was not satisfied with the descriptions of pairs of friends in the drama and novel fragments, as well as the great passages in his January letter and his poem. He was trying with this "literary" piece to put all this into a more nuanced fashion and more concretely. But, alas! it was lost. And I would have been *so* curious to read it!

Bonhoeffer's friendships

1. Friends in the plural

Before offering an interpretation of these sources, a complete treatment of the topic "friendship in Bonhoeffer" would have to describe and characterize his own friendships, which I can do only in brief outline here.

Friendships in the plural appeared in adolescence as soon as 1923 when he moved out of his lively parental home to begin his studies in Tübingen. From then on he brought friends home steadily and without reservation. Before then, I do not know of any long-lasting school friends who remained influential for him. The circle of his many brothers and sisters and their friends met all his needs for stimulation, entertainment and competition.

His studies in Tübingen, his placements in the vicarage in Barcelona (1928), at Union Seminary in New York (1930), at the German parish in London (1933) and at the illegal seminary in Finkenwalde (1935) all brought him friends for hiking and travelling, professional colleagues, fellow lovers of music, like-minded allies and co-experimenters with liturgy and monasticism. His ventures overseas and even attempts to emigrate forged particularly deep bonds; I would mention here Paul and Marion Lehmann, Erwin Sutz and Jean Lasserre.

Finally, the time of the conspiracy created even stronger relationships of trust than the years of the church-struggle. This could be observed in his relationships with Friedrich-Justus Perels and Oscar Hammelsbeck, who belonged to both periods. The prison cell in Tegel brought unique friendships, which had an effect for a long time afterwards, for example with his Italian fellow-prisoner, Professor Gaetano Latmiral. After it was all over, these were simply transferred to me (as was also Paul Lehmann's friendship, from which I enjoyed the richest advantages!). In this connection, I regret that I missed finding and meeting Dietrich's guide through Harlem, Frank Fisher, before he died.

Dietrich's relationships with George Bell and Karl Barth, even the sudden but short-lived nearness to W.A. Visser 't Hooft, deserve special attention. Undoubtedly they became rather like "fatherly friends" for him. Their judgment and understanding were by far the most important for him when he made his weightiest decisions, those regarding the conspiracy. Working for the conspiracy inevitably included abuse of his ecumenical relationships in the service of preparations to topple Hitler. He could not ask any authority within the Confessing Church about that. After 1945 Bell did not hesitate to call the much younger man his friend. For Barth, Bonhoeffer was not the kind of lifelong friend Eduard Thurneysen was, but their relationship went far beyond that between controversial, fascinating dialogue partners.[3]

During the Nazi years, a separate category of friendship was formed in the growing circle of siblings and in-laws. To describe it would require an entire account of the resistance itself, in order to illuminate the combinations of elements of family and friendships. It would reveal a picture of relationships which transcended by far those of a normal family. They had geographical nearness to each other; and their tradition of tending to the pleasurable sides of communicative activities — even when turning points intruded which were anything but pleasurable and in fact brought genuine suffering — was never interrupted. Indeed, it was precisely at those times that they managed to pass on these values to children and grandchildren. All these things became the preconditions for concrete freedom in chains. The flow of information within the family, their competence to give advice and their support systems were all based on the reliability of competent judgment and estimates of the extent to which each one could be burdened for very different kinds of tasks. For example, they thought to organize in advance a procedure for communicating by code in case of imprisonment. Dietrich's parents, nieces and nephews participated in this, and it successfully functioned for a long time.

I am referring here not only to his explicitly friendship-like affinities with the Leibholzes, Schleichers, Dohnanyis and the family of brother Klaus. His relationship to his oldest brother, the physicist Karl-Friedrich, also belongs here, although he lived further away in Leipzig. Dietrich always wanted to account for his professional and faith decisions (in his letters of birthday greetings!) to Karl-Friedrich, particularly as the latter was an agnostic. But in fact among the siblings Karl-Friedrich was the most faithful letter-writer to Dietrich in his Tegel prison cell. Except for the letters from Dietrich's parents, his fiancée and me, the largest number of extent letters from 1943-1944 are from Karl-Friedrich.

Absolute reliability is not an unconditional element of family relationships. But it is one of friendship, and in this they formed a unity, in which family strengthened the friendship element and friendship strengthened the family element.

2. Friends in the singular

Hans Christoph von Hase represents a transition from these family friendships to the "singular friends", of whom there were most likely four. He was a cousin a little more than a year younger than Dietrich, from a country parsonage. His specific relationship to Dietrich was a permanent factor the family took for granted. It continued through long contacts on vacations and by correspondence during childhood through adolescence. It grew more intensive when both of them decided early on to become theologians. Hans Christoph passed on to Dietrich his first notes from Karl Barth's lectures; later, Dietrich passed on to Hans Christoph his fellowship at Union Theological Seminary in New York. The singularity and intensity of their contact lessened when Hans Christoph entered military chaplaincy in 1935 and thus kept a certain distance from the upheaval in the church struggle after the Synod of Dahlem, in which Dietrich was so heavily involved. During the time of the conspiracy, they were in touch only rarely.

A second singular friend was the Berlin pastor and later professor *Walter Dress*. The two were fraternity brothers in the local "Hedgehog" fraternity during Dietrich's first year of university studies in Tübingen. Later he met Dress in the seminars at Berlin University and particularly in the state library. Dress was almost two years older and was already working on his doctoral dissertation, then soon on his second dissertation, the *Habilitation* required to qualify as a university lecturer. The academic and scholarly relationship turned into a family connection when Dress married Dietrich's younger sister Susanne in 1929.

In 1992, during the very week when Volume 10 (documents from the period in Barcelona and the USA) of the new edition of Bonhoeffer's works appeared, we found almost forty more letters and postcards from Dietrich to Walter written between 1925 and 1929. They make clear what a lively theological and literary exchange the two of them had, how they consulted each other and shared their youthful criticisms of the academic and church leaders of the time. The intensity of their exchange receded as Dietrich became involved in the ecumenical world and led a wandering life while Walter remained true to Berlin, and as Dietrich grew to an increasing affinity with Karl Barth during the church struggle, to which Walter was not as sympathetic.

Dietrich's third singular friendship with *Franz Hildebrandt* became all the more intense. Franz was from Berlin, the son of a museum director (for which reason he never entered art galleries in later life). This friendship also began with Harnack's seminars, with sharing their common worries about their dissertations and with lively exchanges of quotations from Luther. Soon thereafter a common passion for the piano appeared. While they did not become in-laws, Franz did soon gain the enduring status of "honorary uncle" for many of Dietrich's own nieces and nephews. Later, as an emigrant to England, Franz always carried photographs in his wallet of the Schleicher and Dohnanyi children in addition to Martin Niemöller's children. The nieces and nephews were often amazed to see the two friends plunge into heated but humorous theological debates, without having any notion of what was meant by the positions of the supposedly "nomian" Dietrich and the supposedly "antinomian" Franz.

With Hitler's rise to power, their joint activities (they had written a catechism together in 1931) took on an increasingly existential dimension. In the fall of 1933 Dietrich took Franz into his parsonage in London, just as his home church, heavily compromised by the Nazis, was about to dismiss him as a "non-Aryan". There they continued their church struggles as well as their music-making. In early 1934 Franz returned to Berlin at Niemöller's request to help in the Dahlem parish and in the Pastor's Emergency League. He emigrated permanently in 1937 after Niemöller was arrested. His emigration brought the daily practice of their friendship to a certain close.

This singular friendship gave Dietrich a partner for abundant dialogue during the time he was working out what became his book *The Cost of Discipleship*, although each friend maintained his own independence in a most productive way. It led to their proving their vocational loyalty to each other during the challenges which brought such profound consequences. It fulfilled the desires of both for humour and satire — for example, Franz wrote a birthday letter to Dietrich in 1934 in the old German style of Martin Luther.[4] It fulfilled their similar musical tastes.

Eberhard Bethge: The friendship between Dietrich Bonhoeffer and me was characterized by the opportunities to live together, of which we took extensive advantage. Even during the time in the early 1940s when I had my own apartment in the Burckhardthaus in Berlin, I lived with him in the Marienburger Allee almost more than in my own place. From 1935 until the end, we also had the bond of our joint illegal status as theologians and pastors of the Confessing Church.

This "friendship of illegals", between an urbane Berliner and a country boy three-and-a-half years younger, was silenced for almost three-quarters of a year when he was arrested on April 5, 1943, during which time I advanced in status to a member of the family by marrying his niece. After the most heated period of interrogation was concluded in November 1943, that amazingly functional smuggled correspondence between us opened up, with the unanticipated consequences which are now available for all to see in the book *Letters and Papers from Prison*. It broke off permanently with Dietrich's transfer to the Gestapo prison in October 1944 and my own imprisonment shortly thereafter. But because I survived, for which he and the family had steered the most important things behind the scenes, our friendship continued in a transformed way.

At first I hesitantly collected and published fragments of his theology (*Ethics*, 1949). Then I secured biographical and historical evidence. In doing so, I involved, so to speak, the whole world in this continuation of our relationship of loyalty. The fruits have long since gone into expert and critical hands from Tokyo to Seattle to Cape Town. And they still unleash new stimulation for people, as they did long ago for me. Michael Trowitzsch of Münster University has explained this in terms of Bonhoeffer's "concentration and passionate insistence on getting to the heart" of the gospel, and this "because here someone is wholeheartedly and passionately and rousingly seeking for what is valid today".[5]

Just as I finished my short account of Bonhoeffer's concrete friendships, I came across some wonderful evidence for this distinction between "plural" and "singular" friendship from Dietrich himself: namely, a few sentences from his birthday in 1941, which he wrote to me at the end of the day from Ettal Monastery in Bavaria. They contain very central thoughts on what friendship really is:

Our letters on the occasion of today are notably similar in their content. This is surely not a coincidence, and confirms that things really are the way it says in the letters. You wished me, among other things, good, stimulating friends. That is a good thing to wish, and today it is a great gift. But the human heart is created in such a way that it seeks and finds refuge in the singular rather than in the plural. That is the claim, the limit and the richness of genuine human relationship, to the extent that it touches on the area of individuality and to the extent that it rests essentially on loyalty. There are individual relationships without loyalty and loyalty without individual relationships. Both are to be found in the plural. But together (which is seldom enough!) they seek the singular, and happy is he who "succeeds in this great luck".[6]

(The "great luck" of the last sentence refers to a line in Friedrich Schiller's famous "Ode to Joy", which Beethoven used in the finale of his Ninth Symphony: *"Wem der grosse Wurf gelungen, eines Freundes Freund zu sein."*)

This letter is a declaration of love from a friend, who rejoices in noting the shape of the relationship and takes pleasure in communicating it in the nocturnal letter to his partner as a wonderful reassurance. He does not attempt any theological or christological derivations, but on the basis of the "last things" which are presupposed he experiences in himself the full freedom of "the things before the last". Thus, he does not have to extrapolate a system from *agape*, from ecclesiological foundations, for example, from Finkenwalde, or from "Life Together",[7] from the "Brethren House"[8] (which of course defines relationships in the plural). This conception flows out of an act of accepting a gift and not from the arduousness of dogmatic logical deductions or from the exegesis of the biblical *philia*.

Therein lies a difference between this 1941 reflection on friendship and that of January 1944 from Tegel prison. The latter is precipitated by certain specific circumstances and issues which force it to seek objectively and decide the place of friendship. Here Bonhoeffer harks back to his own previous systematic attempts at theology and ethics. But he also shows an amazing willingness to call those attempts into question on the grounds of this topic of friendship, which resists being ordered into his analyses. How did it come to this, and what do we hear about it there?

What is friendship?

How did it happen that this genius of giving as well as receiving friendship came so late during his time in Tegel prison to write out such significant reflections on this theme, which order and objectify the facts just related into concepts?

One turning point was the resumption of our communication after the interrogations were finished, an indictment established and hopes high of getting on with the trial. Then he worked on establishing the method of smuggling letters; I even appeared in the prison one day to see him when I was home on leave from the military. At the same time, Dietrich's hopes were raised as never before that he would be able to meet his fiancée in freedom. Nothing came of all that. But an approaching problem came to the surface in the fact that both partners in the friendship would soon be married. This problem does not yet appear in the portrayals of friendship in his attempts at a drama and a novel during the summer and early fall 1943 in Tegel. But after he read the little volume of Stifter, this issue is suddenly present, in a contrast between friendship and family. In that wonderful long first letter of November 18, 1943, he wrote:

> There is so much that I would very, very much like to hear of you! Sometimes I've thought that it is really very good for the two of you [Renate and Eberhard] that I'm not there. At the beginning it's not at all easy to resolve the conflict between marriage and friendship; you're spared this problem, and later it won't exist. But that's only a private and passing thought; you mustn't laugh at it.[9]

The Stifter quotations

In late November a little volume by the Austrian writer Adalbert Stifter was returned from the prison. It was called *Wisdom of the Heart: Thoughts and Observations by Adalbert Stifter. A Breviary* (Berlin, 1941). Dietrich wrote his thanks for it to his parents on November 8:

> Your last parcel was particularly fine. I was very surprised and pleased with the Stifter anthology. As it consists mainly of extracts from his letters, it's almost all new to me.[10]

The return of this little book revealed two bits of rather exciting news for me. First, it signalled a coded message according to the previous agreements in the family, which was to put a tiny pencil mark under one letter every few pages, starting from the back of the book. (The pencil marks were not erased, and are still visible in the remnant of Dietrich's library in my home.) The deciphered message read: "Letter to Eberhard with Wergin." Wergin, a friend of Dietrich's brother Klaus, was the lawyer who was supposed to defend Dietrich in the trial they hoped for. That was the first very long letter of November 18-23, a sudden reopening of the source which had remained tightly sealed for eight months.[11]

Second, we discovered Dietrich's pencil markings at passages about friendship which seemed to speak to our own situation. Here are some sentences from the most important of these:

> A true and upright friend is, next to a loyal wife, the greatest good that a man can have on earth. Our parents are friends given to us by God but, loyal and sincere as they are, they are not born equal with us. Rather they stand over us as recipients of our honour. Thus, our love for them does not dare to come to them with all the little foolishness and trifles with which we bother a friend who is a peer, and in so bothering him find our good fortune with him. A brother is a born friend, but the blood relationship has a sort of right to love. It appears, therefore, as an obligation and does not give the unforeseen joy that love given to us voluntarily by an outsider does. However pure, great or unselfish sibling love is, it does not completely satisfy our existence, and honourable siblings often give it to us even without our doing anything to earn it. Friendship really completes the circle of happiness and gives us (however fine and good the friend really is) the assurance of our own value. An unworthy person has only accomplices, not friends.[12]

Anyone wishing to characterize the dissimilarity between Dietrich's letters to his parents, to his friend and the entirely different third category, the wonderful correspondence to his fiancée from Tegel prison, will find key insights here in Stifter. How important it is for the fullness of life to be able to bother someone with "the little foolishness and trifles", even in a prison cell! We can understand Dietrich's "surprised and pleased" reaction to discovering this and his marking just this passage with his pencil. Unfortunately, he left no notes showing whether he tried to figure out what led Stifter, a Catholic, to come so close to the Lutheran doctrine of orders or to the esteem of friendship in Greek antiquity, transported through nineteen Christian centuries. I have never yet been able to do the work to research this point. In any case, these sentences from Stifter — although they sound outmoded, but full of original experience — do fit the situation of our friendship in November 1943. So they are in accord with and can serve to introduce my further reflections, and they belong necessarily to the following experimental discussion of "mandates".

Letter of January 23, 1944

In mid-December 1943 Dietrich wrote in a letter to me, just at a time when everything was uncertain for me, with the possibility of a military transfer to the Russian or the Italian front:

> You're certainly right in describing marriage as "what remains stable in all fleeting relationships". But we should also include a good friendship among these stable things.[13]

Further complicating this experience of instability was a special problem concerning my following the course of Dietrich's fate with respect to his imprisonment and perhaps forthcoming trial. I had complained to him that his letters to his parents were usually shared immediately with his fiancée Maria and with his brothers and sisters. But only rarely were they ever passed along to his friend. I had written about that to him in Tegel at the New Year 1944. That became the impetus for that great passage in Dietrich's letter about the social, ethical and theological place of the phenomenon of "friendship". In my letter of January 2 from the military base in Lissa, Poland, I had written:

> You write that, after marriage, our friendship is to be counted among the stable things of life. But that is not the case, at least as far as the recognition and consideration by others is concerned. Marriage is recognized outwardly — regardless of whether the relationship between the couple is stable or not; each person, in this case the whole family, must take it into account and finds it the right thing that much should and must be undertaken for it. Friendship — no matter how exclusive and how all-embracing it may be — has no *necessitas*... Your letters of course go to Maria, and almost as automatically to Karl-Friedrich, but it takes an extra struggle to make the point that I have to have them too... In the army, you also say, no one pays any attention to the fact that someone has a very good friend. Friendship is completely determined by its content and only in this way does it have its existence. Marriage does not even need to be that; its formal recognition sustains it... For the sake of my marriage, the family is willing to consider some special efforts on my behalf [for example, how they might influence my being ordered

to Italy instead of to Russia — E.B.]. At the same time, no one has seriously considered how to arrange our possibly being assigned to serve together in case you would come free and at once be called into the army.[14]

This complaint about my lack of participation in the family's information flow from the Tegel cell brought about that letter of January 23, 1944. Later, in 1949, in the first edition of *Ethics*, we integrated the passage from this letter on friendship, its freedom and the possibility or lack thereof as a footnote to his thoughts on the mandates, without describing its place in time and its context.[15] Strangely enough, this passage was not noted or analyzed in the most recent edition of the *Ethics* (*DBW* 6), which was otherwise restructured with the greatest care.[16]

Bonhoeffer's passage on friendship begins with that succinct sentence, for which we now know the cause: "I will also see that you get my letters to my parents."[17] Then follows the experiment with the doctrine of divine mandates[18] from the time that he was writing the fragments of *Ethics* some years earlier. In the experiment, he intended to remain Lutheran while escaping the rigid Lutheran doctrine of orders of creation. We shall see how he came to think that this doctrine of mandates really needed to be revised. One can sense how he wanted to remain flexible, for example in the number of mandates, three or four (or even five?), and how he was really still in the middle of the experiment. Here is the first introductory sentence:

> I think you made a very precise observation in this connection about friendship, which, in contrast to marriage and kinship, enjoys no generally recognized rights, and therefore depends entirely on its own inherent quality.

Thus, Bonhoeffer sees that friendship cannot be defined according to interests, goals and purposes, which could be institutionally codified and then also protected, whether by professions or groups. Rather, it can be defined only by what binding content exists between two people. This content can be very different individually. The different kinds of content give friendships their individual character and intensity. For that reason, they must remain free. They regulate the length of the relation of partnership. Although he does not say this explicitly, that is how I

interpret him, and I think that was how he experienced friendships, in the plural as well as in the singular.

Bonhoeffer then continues: "It is really not easy to classify
friendship sociologically." This conceptual difficulty — or ne-
glect, because it was an unaccustomed project to work on —
stands in contrast to his very practical capacity in his own life to
"classify" his social circumstances with an enduring and influential effect. Compare, for example, his own freedom from
jealousy. Here one should observe the stages of his friendships
through Finkenwalde, through the Brethren House, through the
family, through patterns of behaviour with each of the former
friends.

The letter continues:

> Probably it is to be regarded as a subheading of culture and educa-
> tion, while brotherhood would be a subheading under the concept of
> church, and comradeship a subheading of the concepts of work and
> politics.

Bonhoeffer approaches his topic using a phenomenology of concepts. According to this, friendship is something quite different
from "Finkenwalde" or "Life Together". With the element of
comradeliness Bonhoeffer scarcely associates the military experience; instead, he associates the "political" with the "comradely"
and (as we shall see later) brings that to an impressive climax with
hints of the ongoing risk of responsible conspiracy. Compare,
later, the poem "The Friend" of August 1944.

Now he refers back to his work on the *Ethics* two to four years
earlier:

> Marriage, work, state and church have their concrete divine man-
> date; but what about culture and education?

Back then he had conceived his "doctrine of mandates" in order to
reassure people of their own responsible empowerment in their
positions and decisions, to show them their divine permission
which provides order and to create freedoms. It did all that
without opening the floodgates to the kind of chaos feared by the
Lutherans. Instead, it opened doors for individual creative flexi-
bility. Thus, it showed freedom in obligation. How important the
element of freedom is to him is shown in the continuation of this
passage:

I don't think they can just be classified under work, however tempting that might be in many ways.

Why "tempting"? Because friendship naturally also has to possess a place in the mandate of work, which includes, for example, everything related to the professional. Bonhoeffer surely also has some sense of the widespread criticism against the Lutherans which his doctrine of mandates will attract (for example, from Karl Barth). Therefore, because he is now attempting to locate friendship, we find him clearly stressing how important it is in the mandates to pay attention to the simultaneity which is absolutely necessary: dialectically simultaneous interdependence *and freedom.*

Then follows one of the especially beautiful passages by this experimenting thinker in the prison cell, who always relished playing games (and found fault with me because, besides not speaking English, I knew nothing about chess!). His prison letters are so appealing because they communicate not only his abiding self-control but also his infectious, playful joy, simply "being fully human". So now he is virtually looking for a "fifth" mandate of freedom for the phenomena of culture and education, and with them, also friendship:

> They belong, not to the sphere of obedience, but to the broad area of freedom, which surrounds all three (or four) spheres of the divine mandates. Whoever knows nothing about this area of freedom may be a father, citizen and worker, indeed even a Christian; but I doubt whether he is a complete person (and, thus, a Christian in the widest sense of the term).

There we have what Bonhoeffer was driving at in his ethical theology or theological ethics: "being fully human". There are some passages which epitomize high points of this in the *Ethics* fragments.

Using the example of his own heritage, he then shows that much in this has to be changed:

> Our "Protestant" (not Lutheran) Prussian world has been so dominated by the four mandates that the sphere of freedom has quite receded into the background.

Here we see how Bonhoeffer was unwilling to leave Luther simply to the Lutherans of his century. For him the "Prussian world" extended from the Grunewald neighbourhood in Berlin where he grew up to the eastern Pomerania of his fiancée's extended family, the Kleists.

After this sober analysis there are observations on the hope coming from the recent church struggles, experiences of renewal with enormous implications for the future (which were never realized). He had already mentioned such renewal in his *Ethics*:

> I wonder whether it is possible (it almost seems so today) to regain the idea of the church as providing an understanding of the area of freedom (art, education, friendship, play), so that Kierkegaard's "aesthetic existence" would not be banished from the church's sphere, but would be re-established within it. I really think that is so, and it would mean that we would recover a link with the Middle Ages.

Here Bonhoeffer hints that he is intending to overcome things he misses in those whose mentality is closest to his own in church and theology — the "Kierkegaardians" and Barthians (dialectical theologians) — or rather to fill gaps in "being fully human", and how he intends to do so. This is the concern of some of his *Ethics* sketches. Today, we know more precisely how he was moving in the same direction as the later Karl Barth did at his desk in Basle. Bonhoeffer's discoveries in his analysis and experiments have the particular attraction of having taken place in the midst of his life in the conspiracy and his experiences in the prison cell. Of course, because of that they were often painfully fragmentary, and again and again they were broken off too soon.

In this way, Bonhoeffer remembers experiences just before he was arrested, well aware of how rare they were and how nearly absurd they seemed in the light of Stalingrad and the arrests of the conspirators. He asks about what he himself had just done:

> Who, for instance, in our times can attend to music or friendship, play games or take pleasure in something with an easy mind?

Not long before, in 1942, we had gathered in Berlin-Nikolassee, in the house of Ernst von Harnack, a co-conspirator who later was executed in 1945. There we had celebrated by playing Bach's *Brandenburg Concertos* together. Ernst von Harnack played first flute, I played second flute, Rüdiger Schleicher violin, Emmi

Bonhoeffer viola, Klaus Bonhoeffer cello and Dietrich piano (after he was arrested, Renate took over the piano part). How often that had happened (with a similar distribution of parts) in the Schleichers' house next door to the Bonhoeffers!
Dietrich then answers his own question:

> Surely not the "ethical" person, but only the Christian.

That meant: not the person who rides principles to death and not the moralizer — whose failure Bonhoeffer had described extensively in his essay "After Ten Years" and in his *Ethics*. Rather, it meant someone "fully human", whom he saw created in and through Christ.

And then Bonhoeffer returns from the examples he was remembering to his main line of argument. We see the good Lutheran tersely indicating that he is quite eager to discuss this, and is expecting corrections and further explorations. Note particularly here the especially frequent use of question marks and exclamation points:

> Precisely because friendship belongs to this sphere of freedom ("of the Christian person"!?), it must be confidently defended against all the disapproving frowns of "ethical" existences, though without claiming for it the *necessitas* of a divine commandment, but only the *necessitas* of **freedom**!

Remember that in 1520 Luther wrote that great essay of the Reformation: "On the Freedom of a Christian Person".
With this paradox of a "*necessitas* of **freedom**" Bonhoeffer designates the heart and pivotal point of his "theology of friendship". But we should also note that Dietrich intends that his theology of the mandates should not fall captive to a new rigidity of the Lutheran doctrine of orders, but should be kept open in fruitful illogic. Mandates are in effect, they guide us to take positions, they permit responsible freedoms and, in his understanding, they mean the gospel. But they are not everything! Doesn't Bonhoeffer permit us to tinker with his doctrine of mandates forever after only if we include this passage from January 23, 1944 — that is, if we incorporate this passage on freedom and friendship with the questions it opens anew?

Bonhoeffer closes the outline of his stance with an extraordinary praise of friendship:

> I believe that within the sphere of this freedom friendship is by far the rarest and most priceless treasure, for where else is there any in this world of ours, dominated as it is by the first three mandates [marriage, work, state]? It cannot be compared with the treasures of the mandates; in relation to them it is *sui generis*, but it belongs to them as the cornflower belongs to the grainfield.

At this point we should take a look at the engagement correspondence between Dietrich and Maria von Wedemeyer. During the same weeks in which the phenomenon of friendship had taken hold of him, he mentioned it in his correspondence with Maria. They touch on questions of upbringing in their two families. Dietrich emphasizes, among other things, how good he thinks it is for parents to remain parents and not to try to make themselves "equal" with their children as "friends" in a comradely way. In doing so, he is able to speak very positively about "the austerity in the relationship of a father to a son", and even about a "sanctity of the office of fatherhood".[19] But Maria, whose father had died on the Russian front 18 months earlier, contradicts him very quickly and severely: "I can tell you that I have only ever had one friend, and that was Father."[20] And later: "I cannot completely accept your rejection of friendship with parents... I always took it for granted that when I went riding with Father, I told him *everything.*"[21]

Did she blur Dietrich's "divine orders", maybe even his entire "doctrine of mandates"? Andreas Pangritz of Berlin wrote to me in January 1993 — out of his own pro-Barthian and anti-Lutheran sentiments — what he thinks the 20-year-old girl did to her 38-year-old fiancé: "In the final analysis [she] crossed out the entire doctrine of the mandates. And it seems to me to be no coincidence that Dietrich probably ran out of arguments."

I hardly think that he would have run out of arguments if the couple had been able to continue the discussion. Perhaps he would have admitted that friendship can become a good and useful element in a father-daughter relationship, can even become a particularly fortunate case. As marriage or family and friendship do, perhaps they relate to each other in a complementary way; they may even replace each other in an enriching way.

But in spite of that, friendship and fatherhood are not simply interchangeable. For if their limited interchangeability were always valid or if the one were simply reduced to the other, they would both lose their enriching value for each other and would become poorer.

Statements of the poem from August 1944
   The cornflower in the grainfield — this analogy for friendship within other sociological frameworks takes priority in the second explicitly formulated source on Bonhoeffer's "theology of friendship". It is the word at the moment of the end of the actual practice of the friendship. It takes the concentrated form of a poem, which was a birthday present to me in August 1944.

   By comparison with January of that year, Dietrich's situation had changed fundamentally. In the winter of 1943-1944, there were still expectations of a trial which might turn out positively. The trial was not expected to be conducted by the worst Nazi tribunal or a Gestapo court (although of course the Gestapo would be present), but before the national military court, in which the family could still count on individual judges with whom they had or could establish connections. But now, in August, the assassination attempt against Hitler on July 20, 1944, had failed. With its failure, Dietrich's hopes for his marriage, but also for continuing his underground contacts with friends came to an end.

   Because of all this, the tenor and the intensity of "concentrated" content changes yet again. If his reflection from January 23 could still be valid for friends in the plural, each according to free choice and perception, now he expresses the being and function of a friend almost completely in the singular. From within a deeper entanglement in the conspiracy and its fate he addresses more strongly the "comradely" part of friendship, meaning the parts of complete, reliable loyalty and the acceptance of the possibility of his own sacrifice. This is also harshly and heart-wrenchingly expressed by his short poem "Jonah" from October 1944. Prepared for such sacrifice, and yet filled with comforting, strangely uplifting and certain joy in *philia* just at that moment, the poem contains Bonhoeffer's complete "theology of friendship".[22]

The Friend

1

Not from the heavy soil
where blood and ancestry and oath
are powerful and sacred,
where the earth itself
guards and protects and avenges
the consecrated ancient orders
against madness and wickedness —
not from the heavy soil of earth,
but from free affection
and the spirit's free desires,
needing no oath or legal bond,
friend is given to friend.

2

Beside the wheatfield that feeds us,
which people reverently till and tend,
to which they offer the sweat of their labour,
and if need be,
their bodies' blood;
beside the field of daily bread
people also let
the lovely cornflower bloom.
No one has planted, no one watered it;
it grows, defenceless in freedom,
and in cheerful confidence
that no one will grudge it
life
under the broad sky.
Beside what is needed,
formed from heavy earthly material,
beside marriage, labour, the sword,
the free one wants
to live
and grow towards the sun.
Not the ripe fruit alone —
blossoms are lovely, too.
Do blossoms serve the fruit,
or fruit only serve the blossom —
who knows?

But both are given to us.
Most precious, rarest blossom
— blooming from the freedom of a playing,
daring and trusting
spirit in a happy hour —
is a friend to a friend.

3

Playmates at first
on the spirit's vast journeys
to wonderful,
distant empires;
which, veiled by the morning sun,
gleam like gold;
towards which, in the midday heat,
light clouds in the blue sky
drift;
which, in the stirring night,
tempt the seeker
in the light of the lamp
like hidden secret treasures.

4

When, then, the spirit touches
one's heart and brow
with great, cheerful, bold thoughts,
so that with clear eyes and free bearing
one can face the world;
when, then, the deed springs from the spirit —
the deed, by which each person stands or falls alone —
when from the deed,
strong and healthy,
rises the work
which gives a man's life
content and meaning,
then the acting, working, lonely person
longs for
the befriended and understanding spirit.
Like a clear fresh lake
in which the spirit cleans off the dust of the day,
in which it cools itself from the burning heat
and steels itself in the hour of fatigue —

like a fortress, to which, from danger and confusion,
the spirit returns,
in which it finds refuge, comfort, and strength,
is a friend to a friend.

5

And the spirit longs to trust,
trust without limits.
Disgusted by the mob
that feeds in the shadow of the good
on envy, suspicion and prying,
by the snake-like hissing
of poisoned tongues,
which fear, hate and malign
the mystery of free thought
and upright heart,
the spirit longs
to cast off all deceit
and reveal itself fully
to its kindred spirit,
to ally itself with it freely and loyally.
Ungrudging, it longs to affirm,
longs to acknowledge,
longs to thank,
longs to gain joy and strength
from the other spirit.

6

But it is even willing to bow
to rigorous standards
and rigorous reproach.
The mature man seeks
from the loyalty of his friend
not orders, not binding alien laws and doctrines,
but counsel, good and serious,
which makes him free.

Distant or near,
in joy or in sorrow,
each knows in the other
his loyal helper
to freedom
and humanity.

      * * *

At midnight came the air-raid siren's song;
I thought of you in silence and for long —
how you are faring, how our lives once were,
and how I wish you home this coming year.

We wait till half past one, and hear at last
the signal that the danger now is past;
so danger — if the omen does not lie —
of every kind shall gently pass you by.

The first verse sets "the spirit's free desires" for another spirit meeting it over against the reality, which Bonhoeffer had once described as "orders of preservation" and their laws.

In the second he characterizes the sheer and wonderful "uselessness" of friendship, in which its love lives, just as the cornflower lives uselessly in the middle of the useful cornfield.

The third sings of the playmates of the wander-years.

The fourth describes the longed-for companionship, when loneliness surrounds the irreversible decisions, the deeds and the creative work of the grown-up man.

In the fifth the friend expects the deadly enmity of "poisoned tongues", which call forth the fullness of the functions of an unlimited trust relationship: to "reveal [oneself] fully" to each other, to "affirm", to "acknowledge", to "thank" and "to gain joy and strength from the other spirit".

And the last verse:

Even... rigorous standards... the mature man seeks from the loyalty of his friend... in joy or in sorrow, each knows in the other his loyal helper to freedom and humanity.

That our last source on this topic is a poem such as this makes it clear that Bonhoeffer's "theology of friendship" is not for his part the result of a lecture assignment, worked out at his desk for the next seminar session. But my presentation of course *is* that. This is a lasting difficulty. Be that as it may, it has a place in the chain of my lifelong work, as an answer to his work on a christological theology for being fully human. Here is where it ends, not with conceptual clarification, but with a sermon to himself and to his partner at the moment that the friendship is brought to its end — in order, just because of that end, to resume a transformed life later on.

Several weeks ago I stood with my wife and brother-in-law in the lovely new art museum in Bonn, where there was an exhibition on loan from the Museum of Modern Art in New York. Suddenly we found ourselves standing in front of an oil painting by Max Ernst from 1928, which I had not seen in New York, entitled "The Rendezvous of Friends: The Friends are Transformed into Flowers". On the painting one sees a confusion of brown-red clumps of undefined material. Sticking out of it one can recognize here some ears, there some snakes, a dog's head, teeth, a toad and other such things. Spread above it all are seven very beautiful white rose blossoms. Yes, that is the way it really is: "Friends are transformed into flowers."

NOTES

[1] *LPPN*, pp.192f.
[2] *LPPN*, p.200.
[3] Cf. Rudolf Bohren, *Prophetie und Seelsorge: Eduard Thurneysen*, Neukirchner Verlag, 1982, pp.76-83.
[4] *Gesammelte Schriften*, VI, pp.291ff.
[5] "Auf die Anfänge des Verstehens zurückgeworfen: Bemerkungen zu Dietrich Bonhoeffers Hermeneutik", *Neue Zeitschrift für systematische Theologie*, Vol. 34, No. 3, 1992, p.292.
[6] *Gesammelte Schriften*, II, pp.398f.
[7] Title of the book Bonhoeffer wrote in 1938 on the basis of his three-year experience of teaching and sharing with young vicars in the Finkenwalde seminar.
[8] Brethren House was the residence and meeting place of the vicars' group in Finkenwalde during the years 1935-1938.
[9] *LPPN*, p.131.
[10] *LPPN*, p.125.
[11] *LPPN*, pp.128-38.
[12] Stifter, *op. cit.*, pp.10f.
[13] *LPPN*, p.164.
[14] *LPPN*, p.181.
[15] *Ethics*, first edition, pp.223f.
[16] Cf. A. Pangritz, "Zur Neuausgabe von Bonhoeffers *Ethik*. Erfreuliche Klarstellungen — und eine bedauerliche Unterschlagung", *Weissenseer Blätter*, 5/92, pp.25ff.
[17] *LPPN*, pp.192-93. All following quotations in this passage are from this same source.

¹⁸ Cf. D. Bonhoeffer, *Ethics*, pp. 207ff. By introducing the notion of "mandates", Bonhoeffer intended to provide a new ethical orientation for the basic components of human life and activity: work, marriage, government, church. Traditionally (except for the church), these were understood as "orders of creation"; they had been instituted by God as part of creation and derived their value by being linked back to their origin. For Bonhoeffer, ethics is totally Christ-oriented because in Christ the will of God is fully revealed (and ethics is nothing else but the attempt to do the will of God). Hence the mandates are relevant only "by virtue of their original and final relation to Christ". In other words, work, marriage and government, just like the church, have no intrinsic value apart from the question of how we can do the will of God revealed in Jesus Christ.

¹⁹ Dietrich Bonhoeffer and Maria von Wedemeyer, *Brautbriefe: Zelle 92*, Munich, C.H. Beck Verlag, 1992, p.125.

²⁰ *Ibid.*, pp.128f.

²¹ *Ibid.*, p.134.

²² Written in August 1944 and retranslated using *LPPN*, pp.388f.

Chapter 8

Research — Mediation — Commemoration

Steps to Combat Forgetting

Commemoration renders life human; forgetfulness makes it inhuman. We know of course about the grace of forgetting. But even when remembrance carries grief and shame, it fills the future with perspectives. And the denial of the past furthers the affairs of death, precisely because it focuses exclusively on the present. The degree of accountability regarding yesterday is the measure of a stable tomorrow.

Because the neo-Nazis refuse this accountability they ruin Germany's future. Their clamour for a future that represses Auschwitz is a form of delusion, ending in self-destruction. But anyone who accepts the burden of the past, struggling "against forgetting", will experience a healing scarring-over of the wounds. Scarring, however, makes for mature people.

Blindness

My biography carries the burden of the Shoa. It created the deepest rupture in our history, Christians and non-Christians. What is actually involved?

Most of the time there is talk about our weakness, about our cowardice in the face of Hitler's SA and SS. That was certainly the case. And clearly, the new terrorists are using once more the tactics of intimidation; and there will be no lack of copouts.

But worse than the sins of weakness is the fact of the sin of insensitive strength. Its keyword is blindness. It is a traditional

Address on the occasion of the founding of the association "Gegen Vergessen — für Demokratie", Bonn, November 1, 1993.

blindness which afflicted even the opposition mounted by the Confessing Church against the Third Reich, and of which we are barely free even today — the blindness in which Christians consider themselves the chosen successors of the Jews and the Jews as rejected by God. In this sense Christians were both strong and cowardly, long before those terrible dates of April 1, 1933 (boycott of Jews), September 15, 1935 (Nuremberg laws), November 9, 1938 (pogrom night), January 20, 1942 (Wannsee conference).[1] Our blindness rested on centuries-old creeds and theologies of contempt for Israel, which we robbed of the Bible and of "election" on top of that. And so we were silent on those dates.

And what about this blindness and sterile pride now, half a century later? Its healing — *to see!* — is our theme. This for me is at the heart of the commitment that has led to the formation of this association "Against Forgetting". Obviously, this involves a long and strenuous process, with many ups and downs, with disappointing and encouraging moments. Dates and names have to be recalled, ways of seeing have to be connected, controversies have to be faced.

I shall come back to the fundamental task we face by establishing the association "Against Forgetting", but first I should like to recall a few experiences, complicated encounters to be endured on our way, which make it urgent for us to unite and to support, activate and counsel one another in what we are attempting here today.

Fifteen years ago my wife and I attended a conference on the Holocaust in San Jose, California. The article my wife wrote about it later in *Evangelische Kommentare* was entitled "A Hard Conference to Endure". At that time, the term "Holocaust" (from the Old Testament, meaning "total burnt offering") was still unknown as a designation for what had happened at Auschwitz. Since then the film of the same name has made it well-known, thus enabling people to develop certain perspectives on what had happened and to start raising awareness.

Half the participants at the meeting in San Jose were US Christians who were conscious of their involvement in that inherited blindness, for which they coined the term "theology of contempt". The other half were Jews from the USA, Canada and Israel, among them world famous scholars such as Emil Fackenheim, Bruno Bettelheim and Raul Hilberg.

At one point we spoke about the developments leading up to July 20, 1944, and the tormenting logic of conspiratorial resistance. We mentioned that conspirators had to be prepared to collaborate even with officers of the SS, for example, Wolf Count von Helldorf, then in the Central Security Office of the Reich (RSHA), who had earlier been involved in actions connected with the "final solution" in Poland. Now he was a co-conspirator, ready to quit RSHA but induced by Hans Oster and Hans von Dohnanyi to keep his post there under all circumstances. Helldorf was betrayed and paid with his life on September 10, 1944.

But we found no understanding whatever for such events among Hilberg and his friends. No, they said, July 20, 1944, means nothing for Jews. Yet our having participated in that conspiracy was why we had been invited to this conference, a conference devoted to informing about German actions, the evil ones as well as the few good ones. However, our important dates met with conscious indifference on the part of those eminent Jews. And, indeed, the failed and belated plot had changed nothing for their desperate situation. But they did not even grant that some members of the resistance, as we had mentioned, had taken risks for their — the Jews' — sake. They interrupted us, saying, "Well, that's what they call resistance; at the same time, they still murdered the Jews; many of them wanted to keep the concentration camps; of course, once they saw that the war was lost they wanted to do something."

What should we say? Deny what we did? Forget it? My wife and I were the only Germans and the only Lutherans there. Should we have argued that at least the two of us did not belong to the evildoers, with four members of my wife's family (Klaus and Dietrich Bonhoeffer, Rüdiger Schleicher and Hans von Dohnanyi) having been murdered by the Nazis? No! This is precisely what Dietrich Bonhoeffer opposed when he said that "guilt must be confessed without looking sideways at other possibly guilty ones".[2] It would also break off conversations that are yet to begin. As Lutherans we could hardly point to martyrs, unlike the Polish Catholics, who mourn thousands of victims in concentration camps. At that time statements of our church like the 1980 Bad Neuenahr declaration of the synod of the Rhineland church on "The Renewal of Relations between Christians and Jews" were not yet available; there the point was finally made that there was no need for Jews to revise their Torah, but that there was need for Christians to revise their creeds and the decisions of their councils and synods.

But other things also happened to us at San Jose which we shall not forget. On the first evening a Jewish student whom we had met in Berkeley came up to us and said: "I thought of you all day, how terrible it must be for you to hear all this. But I know that not all Germans were that terrible. I just wanted to tell you." At the end of the conference he came to say good-bye: "I shall tell my parents that Germans are like other people, and that I shall no longer participate in boycotting them." We have not seen each other since. Does he still maintain his view after Rostock and Solingen?[3] I dare to think of Ignaz Bubis![4] How would he react to our undertaking here? Will we be believed as we engage in the long and difficult process "against forgetting"?

One more incident. At the table next to us sat a history professor from Haifa, formerly from Berlin, never saying a word. My wife wrote of her: "I felt strongly her reserve. When I did not applaud after my husband's presentation she whispered to me: 'I never applauded either when my husband spoke.' At the end of the meeting we exchanged addresses."

I wish that something similar might take place as a result of this association coming into being. Exchange of addresses! In a given situation this can mean a lot. But it remains an isolated act unless it is sustained by imagination and continuous efforts.

The third generation

We can never get rid of our recent history. Not even the third or fourth generation after the Holocaust can do that. In fact, we must insist that the call "against forgetting" also concerns them. They are not guilty in the same sense as are we, the contemporaries. Nevertheless, the Hitler years are part of their history and in this sense an inescapable part of their identity. One needs only to have lived abroad to realize that the mention of Germany does not necessarily remind people exclusively of Bach and Goethe. To suppress the terrible parts of German history is to deceive oneself and others.

Even innocent members of the third and fourth generation can become guilty, depending on how they deal with the heritage of the Shoa, how they pass it on or whether they remain silent about it. They are co-responsible for the effort to "teach the holocaust", as they say in the United States. This is a far-reaching task which will also have to be shouldered by this association. To say that this does not concern us would only be another way of becoming guilty, entailing fatal consequences: first suppression of the past; but then, since it ultimately cannot be suppressed, defamation, arson and finally murder. As we said already, forgetting the past renders life inhuman; but accepting the burden of the past leads to the experience of the scarring over of the wounds.

Research, mediation, commemoration

Both the contemporaries and the later generation will therefore have to assume the never-ending task of this association, a task confronting every humane German: "against forgetting". The task is threefold: research, mediation, commemoration.

Each of these areas requires its own logic and method, and each will degenerate to the extent to which the other two are not functioning or are excluded. Each will have its own and sometimes willful supporters, but each must want to be corrected by the work of the other two dimensions and carries part of the responsibility for them. If the founding of our association today is to mean anything, it has to engender the commitment "against forgetting" in all three dimensions, in order to achieve clarity about who we are and especially about who we are not.

1. Research aims at solid and informed knowledge. It secures the sources without leaving out the disagreeable parts. It resists the temptation to streamline the tradition according to the motto, "to determine what has happened is to determine what will be". One book is already available, *Die neue deutsche Ideologie. Einsprüche gegen die Entsorgung der Vergangenheit*, by Jürgen Ebach. He presents a "remembrance against the utilization of history". One of the main tasks of this association seems to me to be calling attention to this problem and seeking resources to deal with it.

2. In the second area we have to deal with the past in almost the opposite way. Here it is not a matter of presenting every source but of choosing and setting emphases, of omitting this or that, in order to set out the essence of what has to be presented of that past. This is the job of parents and teachers, of authors, film directors and playwrights, of photographers and poets, of

prophets and pastors, of journalists and comedians. The risk of taking sides is called for; it must be faced by each father and mother when the children start asking questions. How often we hear: "My parents never told me about it, never answered when I asked."

3. The third way of dealing with this history is its commemoration. This is still more than merely remembering. It is an act of vital meditation, a "liturgy" to be performed by individuals, groups and the nation, in the context of the church, society and the state. There is no life without its calendar. There are places, stones, graves, documents, dates and gatherings. These are the moments for new commitments. What has been identified through research and mediation can lead to new identifications. Things are renounced and others are promised; we say No to some and Yes to others. Commemoration reaches out for a renewed world. It no longer looks for forgiveness as the opium for the unresolved issues but it confronts that which can never be resolved by accepting the purifying judgment. The act of commemoration presupposes the knowledge that reconciliation can never be initiated, neither by the perpetrators nor by the victims, as it was stated a few years ago by Israel's President Chaim Herzog in Bergen-Belsen, in the presence of German President Richard von Weizsäcker. This is to be expected, because it is not a question of siblings ending a longstanding fight, but of Cain having killed Abel and having to live with it — and being allowed to do so.

Three approaches are envisioned by our act of founding this association: curiosity combined with cool objectivity; subjective imagination; and the emotion of creative shame.

Archives, lexicons and seminars are one thing; the stage, the screen, the pulpit and the academy, the novel of resistance and the passing on of knowledge within a family are another; and the manifestation on the Hill of Ashes[5] in Flossenbürg, taking an oath and rendering honour in front of the wall in the Stauffenbergstrasse,[6] and worship in the hangman's shed of Plötzensee are the third.

All three practices together form the whole. Our founding act expresses our commitment to all three. We shall have to deal with the respective specialists in each area. This is natural, for they not only limit and contest one another; they inevitably challenge and enrich each other.

Thus, our particular past, which we must not and should not forget, will become our heritage, despite the popular wish and the terrorist campaigns. It will be a redeeming heritage which we, unlike the neo-Nazis, do not suffocate, and which will therefore not suffocate us either, but build us up and offer us space to breathe.

NOTES

[1] At a meeting in Wannsee, Berlin, in January 1942, the top leadership from the government and the party worked out the strategy for executing Hitler's order of a "final solution" — the eradication of the Jews within German-dominated Europe.

[2] *Ethics*, p.118.

[3] Two German cities which achieved notoriety in 1993 because of attacks by neo-Nazi groups on buildings there where foreigners were housed.

[4] President of the Jewish Council of Germany.

[5] The site in Flossenbürg where Bonhoeffer's remains are believed to be buried.

[6] Headquarters of the German Central Military Command (OKW) during the second world war. It was also the site of secret meetings of the conspirators, as well as of the execution of many of them on the day following the failed assassination attempt of July 20, 1944. For this reason it was, in 1994, the site of the "official" fiftieth anniversary commemoration of the attempt.